NATIONS OF THE WORLD

KENYA

Bridget Giles

RAINTREE
STECK-VAUGHN
PUBLISHERS

A Harcourt Company

Austin   New York
www.steck-vaughn.com

Steck-Vaughn Company

First published 2002 by Raintree Steck-Vaughn Publishers,
an imprint of Steck-Vaughn Company.
Copyright © 2002 Brown Partworks Limited.

Library of Congress Cataloging-in-Publication Data

Giles, Bridget
    Kenya / Bridget Giles.
       p. cm -- (Nations of the world)
    Includes bibliographical references (p.) and index.
    ISBN 0-7398-1290-4
    1. Kenya-- Juvenile literature. [1. Kenya.] I. Title. II. Nations of the world (Austin, Tex.)

DT433.522.G55 2001
967.62--dc21

2001019505

Printed and bound in the United States
2 3 4 5 6 7 8 9 0   05 04 03

Brown Partworks Limited
Project editor: Peter Jones
Designers: Seth Grimbly Joan Curtis
Cartographers: Colin Woodman and
    William Le Bihan
Picture Researcher: Lizzie Clachan
Editorial Assistant: Anthony Shaw
Indexer: Kay Ollerenshaw

Raintree Steck-Vaughn
Publishing Director: Walter Kossmann
Art Director: Richard Johnson
Editor: Shirley Shalit

Front cover: Overview of Rift Valley
(background); Samburu woman (below right);
carved rhino (top left)
Title page: Peaks of Mount Kenya

Contents

Foreword

S ince ancient times, people have gathered together in communities where they could share and trade resources and strive to build a safe and happy environment. Gradually, as populations grew and societies became more complex, communities expanded to become nations—groups of people who felt sufficiently bound by a common heritage to work together for a shared future.

Land has usually played an important role in defining a nation. People have a natural affection for the landscape in which they grew up. They are proud of its natural beauties—the mountains, rivers, and forests—and of the towns and cities that flourish there. People are proud, too, of their nation's history—the shared struggles and achievements that have shaped the way they live today.

Religion, culture, race, and lifestyle, too, have sometimes played a role in fostering a nation's identity. Often, though, a nation includes people of different races, beliefs, and customs. Many may have come from distant countries. Nations have rarely been fixed, unchanging things, either territorially or racially. Throughout history, borders have changed, often under the pressure of war, and people have migrated across the globe in search of a new life or because they are fleeing from oppression or disaster. The world's nations are still changing today: Some nations are breaking up and new nations are forming.

The land now covered by modern Kenya is one of the earliest areas of human habitation and for many thousands of years was farmed by hunter gatherer peoples. On the coast a distinctive Swahili culture developed starting in the eighth century A.D. In the 15th century the region became subject to foreign rule, which was to continue in different forms until independence in 1963. Since then Kenya has developed as one of the most successful and stable African economies, its exports based on agriculture, particularly tea, coffee, and cut flowers. To the outside world, however, Kenya is perhaps most remarkable for the splendor of its flora and fauna and the variety of its tropical terrain.

Introduction

Kenya is a country of great beauty and many surprises. Perhaps a typical image of Kenya for many people includes a herd of zebra grazing or stampeding across grasslands, accompanied by antelope and chased by lions. Yet an equally typical Kenyan scenery might include snowcapped mountains, scorching deserts, bustling cities that are home to international organizations, and historic towns founded hundreds of years ago.

Kenya lies in east Africa, bordering the Indian Ocean. Its neighbors are Sudan, Somalia, and Ethiopia to the north and Tanzania to the south; Uganda lies to the west, sharing with Kenya part of the shoreline of Lake Victoria, Africa's largest lake.

Today Kenya is one of east Africa's most stable and wealthy nations, though it has been held together by one-party rule for many years. It has a thriving manufacturing sector, the most well-developed in the whole region. While the vast majority of Kenyans support themselves by farming or breeding animals, thousands also work in offices in cities, teach at universities, or serve in the armed forces.

In terms of the world economy, Kenya is small. However, its position and its economic prosperity give the country advantages over its neighbors. Because of its political importance, Nairobi, Kenya's capital, was chosen as the site of the United Nations' regional headquarters.

The Fourteen Falls at Thika outside Nairobi plunge about 100 feet (33 m) over a precipice. After heavy rains they form one gigantic sheet of water.

FACT FILE

- Kenya is not one of east Africa's largest countries. At 224,903 square miles (582,650 sq. km), it is roughly twice the size of Nevada, and only half the size of Ethiopia, its east African neighbor.

- Many Kenyans refer to the country's different ethnic groups as "tribes." This term does not have the negative associations for Africans as it does for Native Americans. Kenyan and other African ethnic groups often number in the millions and have histories thousands of years old.

- Lake Victoria is the source of the world's longest river, the Nile.

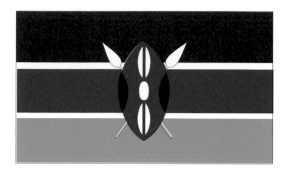

The Kenyan flag features the shield of the Maasai warriors. The black stands for the people, green for the land, red for the price of freedom (blood), and white for peace in Kenya.

The Kenyan shilling is based on the old British unit of currency.

MULTIETHNIC SOCIETY

The Maasai warrior is another familiar image of Kenya. Although the Maasai's way of living is fascinating, they are but a tiny minority, numbering only around 400,000, of Kenya's 30 million plus citizens. Over hundreds of years, many different peoples have migrated from all over Africa, the Middle East, Asia, and Europe to live in what is now Kenya. Today, there are more than 40 recognized ethnic groups. Each has its own language, religion, culture, and history.

The largest ethnic groups in Kenya are the Kikuyu, numbering more than 4.5 million, closely followed by the Luo and Kalenjin at around 2.5 million each. The Kikuyu, Luo, and other predominantly farming peoples are concentrated in the south, center, and southwest of the country. Ranging widely over the arid (dry) and semiarid regions of more northerly regions live Samburu, Turkana, Somali, and Oromo people, who typically make a living from keeping herds of cattle. Not all Kenyans are ethnically African. Small but influential communities of Indians, Arabs, and Europeans are concentrated in the towns and cities. Around 100,000 Kenyans are of part-Asian, generally Indian, descent. Most Asian Kenyans live in Nairobi.

It is not possible to tell which ethnic group a person belongs to by their appearance or dress. One person may be related to people from several different ethnic groups. While some people trace their roots through their father, others do so through their mother, or even their mother's brother.

POPULATION DENSITY

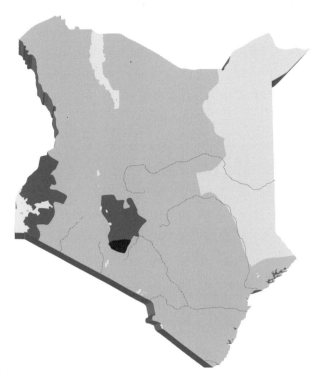

Kenya's population is concentrated in the west of the country near Lake Victoria and in the Central Highlands around Nairobi. The dry plains to the north are inhabited largely by nomadic peoples, who move on when the land or rivers dry up. Increasingly, however, governments have encouraged nomads to settle in one place.

PERSONS

Per sq. mi		Per sq. km
13		5
130		50
780		300
1160		500

Improvements in health care since independence from Britain in 1963 have led to a dramatic increase in population.

Multilingual Citizens

Most Kenyans speak at least two languages fluently, and many speak more. In addition to the language spoken by their parents, Kenyans learn Swahili. School lessons are taught in Swahili. It is also used for news and radio broadcasts and is common in Kenya's cities. Swahili is derived from the Arabic word for "of the coast." The Swahili people themselves live mostly along the coast, but their language has spread into the entire region over many centuries. At first it was a trading language, used by merchants from different lands as a common tongue. Today, Swahili is the common

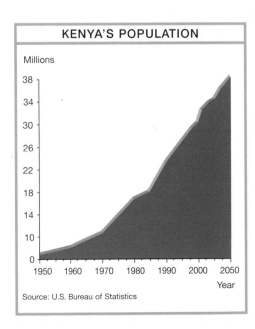

KENYA'S POPULATION

Millions

Source: U.S. Bureau of Statistics

9

Speaking the same language unites people socially and culturally, and it is language that often defines an ethnic group. Kenyan languages, and ethnic groups, fall into three main groups: Bantu, Nilotic, and Cushitic.

language spoken by all Kenyans, and other east Africans, whatever their native tongue. For this reason it was declared the official language of Kenya in 1974. People in Kenya, Tanzania, Uganda, Rwanda, Burundi, and parts of Zambia, Zimbabwe, Democratic Republic of Congo (Zaire), and Somalia all speak Swahili.

Swahili is an adaptable language. Many words have been adopted from Arabic, Persian, European, and Indian languages, and the language continues to change. On the streets of Nairobi, a new street language called Sheng is emerging, which consists of Swahili with words from other African languages and English thrown in. It began in the poor inner-city areas of Nairobi, but is now being used by many levels of society.

The third language that many Kenyans speak fluently is English. This is the country's other official language and it is the language of offices and parliament. Students are taught in English as teenagers and at universities, and it is the language of city business.

POPULATION

Toward the end of the 20th century, Kenya's population growth rates were very high. In 1980, every Kenyan woman was mother to an average of eight children. Such high fertility rates would have more than doubled Kenya's population every 20 years. Large families have been preferred for a variety of reasons, as they were in Europe and North America until the 20th century. Many children died young, and parents had more children so that their offspring would provide for them and care for them as they grew older. As standards of living and health care have improved, large families have become less and less necessary. In Kenya, government

POPULATION BY AGE

%	
51.3	0–15 yrs
26.5	15–29 yrs
12.7	30–44 yrs
6.3	45–59 yrs
3.2	60+ yrs

Source: *Britannica Online*

ETHNIC COMPOSITION

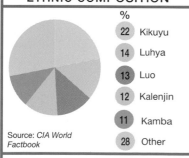

%	
22	Kikuyu
14	Luhya
13	Luo
12	Kalenjin
11	Kamba
28	Other

Source: *CIA World Factbook*

RELIGIOUS PERSUASION

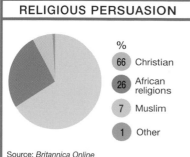

%	
66	Christian
26	African religions
7	Muslim
1	Other

Source: *Britannica Online*

WHERE DOES KENYA'S POPULATION LIVE?

28%
Cities and towns

72%
Country

There are more than 29 million people living in Kenya. At least 70 percent live on just 10 percent of the country's land: in the coastal regions, in western Kenya, near Lake Victoria, and in the Central Highlands. Twenty-eight percent live in urban areas, mostly in the capital city, Nairobi, and in Mombasa on the coast.

campaigns to promote family planning hastened the decline in family size. By 1997, the average fertility rate in Kenya had fallen to 4.5 children per adult woman.

RELIGION

About 66 percent of Kenyans are Christian, either Roman Catholics or followers of one of Kenya's independent Protestant churches. There are more than 30,000 Muslims in Kenya. Many Kenyan Muslims are Ismailis, a group led by the Aga Khan. He has important business and charity links with east Africa, particularly with Kenya. In addition, Kenya has several thousand Hindus, Sikhs, and Jains—these are followers of Indian religions.

The National Anthem

Kenya's national anthem was composed by a national commission of citizens. The melody is traditional and is based on a Kenyan folk song. The anthem was adopted in 1963.

O God of all creation,
Bless this our land and nation.
Justice be our shield and defender,
May we dwell in unity,
Peace, and liberty.
Plenty be found within our borders.

Let one and all arise
With hearts both strong and true.
Service be our earnest endeavor,
And our homeland of Kenya,
Heritage of splendor,
Firm may we stand to defend.

Let all with one accord
In common bond united,
Build this our nation together,
And the glory of Kenya,
The fruit of our labor
Fill every heart with thanksgiving.

Land and Cities

"Beads around my neck, Mt. Kenya away
Over pineappled hills, Kikuyuland. A book of poems.
Mt. Kenya's bluish peaks 'Wangara!' My new name."

From *African Images—Glimpses from a Tiger's Back* by
African-American novelist and poet, Alice Walker

Covering an area of some 224,903 square miles (582,650 sq. km), Kenya includes a wide range of different terrains, from the tropical swamps of the eastern coast to the cool mountains of its center. From north to south Kenya is divided in two by the equator, while from east to west the country is divided by the Rift Valley, a huge depression in the earth's crust that stretches from Jordan to Mozambique. This central region is characterized by the extinct volcanoes of Mount Kenya and Mount Elgon and by shallow lakes that attract a huge variety of birdlife, many of which stay the winter in the country. The Central Highlands are a cooler fertile region with frequent rainfall, where cash crops such as tea, coffee, and, more recently, cut flowers are grown. In the country's north are vast tracts of semiarid land and just east of Lake Turkana in the far north lies the Chalbi Desert. These areas are sparsely populated by nomadic people who cross the plains in search of water and vegetation for their livestock. To the west Lake Victoria links Kenya with the rest of Central Africa, and it is through this hot, humid region that much of the trade of east Africa travels on its way to the tropical eastern coast. Kenya's diverse range of different climates gives the country one of the richest animal populations anywhere in the world.

The sleepy Swahili town of Lamu on Kenya's east coast is the country's oldest and was already a thriving center by the 16th century.

FACT FILE

- Kenya's international borders cut across cultural and historical boundaries. For example, the Oromo and Somali people to the north once called a much larger area home, but their territories have been divided between the modern-day states of Kenya, Ethiopia, and Somalia. To the south, a similar fate befell the Maasai, whose lands were split between Kenya and Tanzania.

- Millions of wildebeest travel across Kenya every year.

- More than half of Kenya's forests have been destroyed in the last 100 years.

KENYA'S TERRAIN

Arid plains
Northwest Kenya is characterized by arid plains and one area of real desert, the Chalbi Desert. In the center of this area is Lake Turkana, formed, like many of Kenya's other lakes, on the floor of the Rift Valley.

Coastal plains
The area east of the Central Highlands is mainly savanna, which toward the coast becomes tropical swampland.

The Central Rift
The Central Rift (*see* p. 17), which splits the Central Highlands, has volcanoes, lakes, hot springs, and scrubby savanna.

Central Highlands
Kenya's uplands enjoy ample rainfall and a more temperate climate than the rest of the country. The peaks of Mount Kenya are covered in snow all year.

TERRAIN

Kenya has virtually the whole sweep of environments, from deserts to snowcapped mountains, from tropical beaches to lush green highlands. The eastern border is made up of 526 miles (846 km) of Indian Ocean coast. Spectacular beaches of white sand lined by coconut palms, sheltered coves, and clear, blue waters are typical of this tropical coast and the small islands that nestle scattered along the shore. Offshore, coral reefs form a barrier along the coast.

Grassland to Desert

The land rises gently from the coast. Behind the narrow strip of fertile coastal lowlands, which is ten to 100 miles (16 to 160 km) wide, are dry, waterless lands called *nyika*. Thornbush, acacia trees, elephant grass,

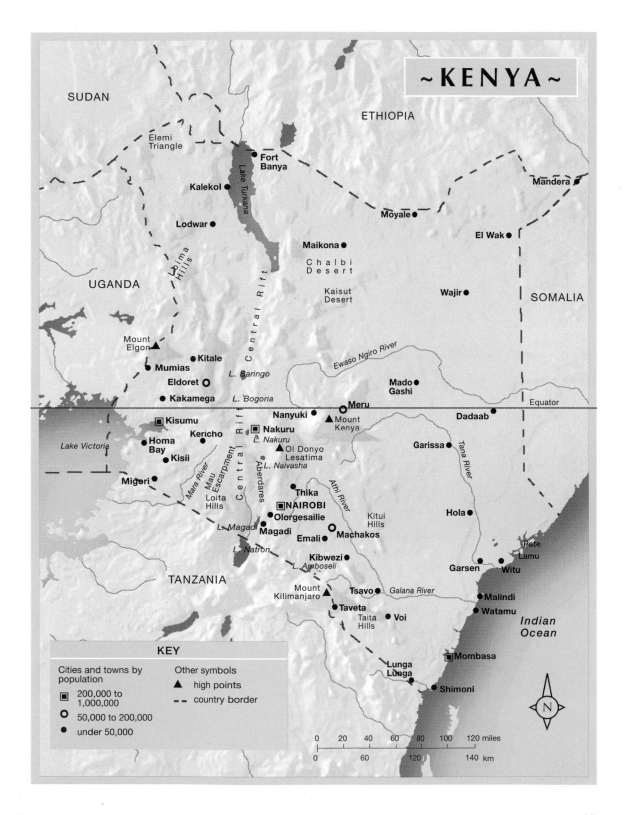

~ KENYA ~

SUDAN

ETHIOPIA

Elemi
Triangle

Lake Turkana

● Fort
Banya

● Mandera

Kalekol ●

Moyale ●

● El Wak

Lodwar ●

● Maikona

C h a l b i
D e s e r t

UGANDA

Kaisut
Desert

● Wajir

SOMALIA

Dolma Hills

Central Rift

▲ Mount
Elgon

● Kitale

Mumias ●

Eldoret ○

● Kakamega

L. Baringo

L. Bogoria

Ewaso Ngiro River

Mado ●
Gashi

Equator

● Meru

Nanyuki ●

▲ Mount
Kenya

● Dadaab

■ Kisumu

Kericho ●

Lake Victoria

Homa
Bay ●

● Kisii

Migori ●

Mara River

Mau Escarpment

Central Rift

Aberdares

Loita
Hills

■ Nakuru
L. Nakuru

▲ Ol Donyo
Lesatima

L. Naivasha

● Garissa

Tana River

Thika ●

■ NAIROBI

● Olorgesailie

L. Magadi
Magadi ●

Emali ●

○ Machakos

Kitui
Hills

● Hola

Athi River

L. Natron

Kibwezi ●

L. Amboseli

TANZANIA

Mount
Kilimanjaro ▲

Tsavo ●

Galana River

Garsen ●

Witu ●

Pate
Lamu

● Malindi
● Watamu

Indian
Ocean

Taveta ●

Taita
Hills

● Voi

Lunga
Lunga ●

■ Mombasa

● Shimoni

KEY

Cities and towns by
population

■ 200,000 to
   1,000,000

○ 50,000 to 200,000

● under 50,000

Other symbols

▲ high points

--- country border

N

| 0 | 20 | 40 | 60 | 80 | 100 | 120 miles |

| 0 | | 60 | | 120 | | 140 km |

and the strangely shaped baobab tree are among the few plants that grow taller than a person. All can survive without water for some time. The more deeply rooted trees tap moisture lying far beneath the surface. The baobab stores water in its grossly swollen trunk, out of which jut spindly branches. Short, tough grasses flourish when the rains come, but die down when the rains fail. Buds lie dormant beneath the dry topsoil, ready to spring back to life as soon as the rains return. These plains become increasingly dry to the north, and increasingly wet toward the inland center of Kenya. Much of northern and northeastern Kenya is semidesert, where vegetation is sparse and limited to hardy thornbushes, acacias, Boswellia, palms, cactuslike euphorbias, and a few temporary patches of grass. The fragrant gum frankincense is harvested from Boswellia trees. Kenya's one true desert—the Chalbi Desert—is in the north of the country, to the east of Lake Turkana. In the grasslands and semideserts, generally the only agriculture practiced is animal herding. Rainfall is not reliable enough for farming.

Central Highlands to Lake Shore

Scattered hills are islands of fertility in the dry, grassy plains, particularly in the south and southeast of Kenya. The Taita, Kasigui, and Kitui hills are among the highest clusters. Even farther inland, the center of

Mount Kenya (below) is revered by the Kikuyu and other peoples as the dwelling place of the supreme god, Ngai.

Kenya is continuous highlands and flat plateaus, leading west to the part of the Great Rift Valley that Kenyans call the Central Rift. With their nutrient-rich volcanic soils, these lands are the most fertile in Kenya, and they are intensively farmed by the mainly Kikuyu inhabitants. Tea, coffee, pine, and eucalyptus grow in the higher regions. Oranges, bananas, pineapples, and corn thrive farther down the slopes.

Dense forests of bamboo circle the higher peaks, sometimes merging upward into forests of giant heather. Lower slopes bear forests of cedar, olive, and other hardwood trees. Beneath the mountain forests, pine and cypress trees might be planted and harvested to make paper, furniture, or timber for houses. In the misty moorlands on high plateaus and mountain slopes, mutant alpine plants such as groundsel and lobelia (*see* p. 29) grow more than 20 feet (6 m) tall.

The Central Rift

The Great Rift Valley cuts Kenya in half from north to south, separating the lower plains of the east from the highlands in the west. This massive gash in the planet's surface has been forming for 30 million years. Earth's crust is made of plates of solid rock, and the plates on which Africa and Arabia sit are moving slowly apart, splitting at the Rift Valley. In Kenya, the Central Highlands were formed by molten rock (lava) spewing from this rift, which divides a great raised dome of land. Inactive volcanoes such as Mounts Kenya and Elgon, as well as smaller active volcanic islands in Lake Turkana, in northern Kenya, are reminders of how the rift formed. There is still some underground volcanic activity, and numerous hot springs, steam jets, and geysers bubble up or erupt from beneath the valley floor.

Before the arrival of the Europeans, the dramatic landscape of the Rift Valley had for centuries been dominated by the forefathers of the Maasai.

The entire Great Rift Valley stretches some 4,000 miles (6,400 km) from the Jordan River in the Middle East to Mozambique in southern Africa. The main valley averages 30 to 40 miles (48 to 64 km) wide. Plateaus either side slope up toward the valley lip, then drop sharply up to 3,000 feet (900 m) to the valley floor. Along the Mau Escarpment (a long cliff or steep slope), the drop can be more than 9,000 feet (2,700 m).

West of the southern half of the Central Rift, the highlands descend into rolling hills then flat lowlands, which border the northeast shores of Africa's largest lake, Lake Victoria. These lands, inhabited by the Luo, Nandi, Kipsigis, Luhya, and other peoples, are also heavily farmed. Tea and sugar crops cover the rolling hills to the southwest.

Kenya's Lakes

Where parts of the valley floor have become covered with water, lakes have formed. This is particularly the case in the Rift Valley, which runs down the center of the country. With no outlet to the sea, the waters of Lake Turkana in north Kenya are brackish, or salty. Although it also has no outlet,

El Molo cattle feed on weeds growing in Lake Turkana in northern Kenya.

the waters of Lake Naivasha, which lies between the cities of Nakuru and Nairobi, are kept fresh by rainwater. Lake Baringo, to the north of Nakuru, is the only other freshwater lake in the Central Rift. Kenya's other five lakes are soapy soda (sodium carbonate) lakes like Magadi, southwest of Nairobi. Hot streams carrying soda flow into these lakes, dyeing them pink. Springs of water laden with sodium gush up through the lake's dry crust. Today the lakes are widely used for chemical extraction (*see* p. 87).

Kenya's Rivers

Kenya has few rivers. In the highlands, they cascade down steep slopes and plunge over waterfalls. Millions of years ago a huge dome of land sat in west-central Kenya. This dome became the Central Rift, and rivers drained eastward from it into the Indian Ocean and westward to the Atlantic Ocean or Congo River. Today, rivers to the west drain into Lake Victoria. The Tana, Athi, and Galana Rivers follow the ancient pattern, rising in the Central Highlands and flowing toward the Indian Ocean.

Kenya's longest river, the Tana, flows through the east of the country. The last 150 miles (240 km) of the river run through marshland.

Provinces and Districts

Kenya is divided into eight provinces. Each has a capital and a provincial governor. The provinces are divided into anything from two districts, in the case of Coast Province, to 14 districts, in the case of Rift Valley

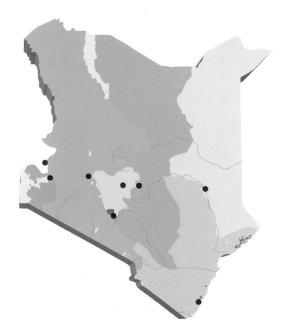

THE PROVINCES OF KENYA

Each of Kenya's eight provinces has a fairly distinct geographical terrain. The capital of each region is indicated on the map on the left with a dot. The regions and their capitals are listed below.

- NAIROBI AREA Nairobi
- CENTRAL Nyeri
- COAST Mombasa
- EASTERN Embu
- NORTH-EASTERN Garissa
- NYANZA Kisumu
- RIFT VALLEY Nakuru
- WESTERN Kakamenga

19

Province. Nairobi Province is not divided into districts. Nairobi is the smallest province, but is also the most populous, with around 3 million inhabitants. The Eastern and Rift Valley Provinces take up the greatest area of Kenya. The North East Province, another of the larger provinces, is home to the lowest number of people. Most of the land is dry grasslands and semidesert scrub.

Central and Western Provinces are primarily used for farming. The Eastern Province is the most varied in Kenya, with landscapes ranging from near-deserts in the north to grasslands to the south. Animal herding is most common in Eastern and Rift Valley Provinces. Nyanza is the Swahili word for lake, and Nyanza Province lies on the shores of Lake Victoria, which Kenya shares with Uganda and Tanzania. Many fishers live there.

THE PERFECT CLIMATE

In Kenya, rainfall varies with temperature since most areas are warm to hot all year long, except at night. It can get cold on the grasslands after sunset, and the summits of Mounts Kenya and Elgon are below freezing at night. Although the Central Highlands are near the equator, the altitude cools the climate, making it more comfortable. Indeed, the climate of the Central Highlands has been described as nearly perfect: sunny days followed by cool nights, with plenty of rain.

Trade Winds

The tropical Kenyan coast has a monsoon climate. Monsoons are seasonal winds that reverse direction roughly every six months, resulting in two seasons: one wet and one dry. They always blow from cooler to warmer lands. In Kenya, they blow toward land from the sea in summer (November to April), bringing rain. Winters are cooler and drier, and the winds blow away from the land toward the sea from May to October. The monsoon winds have not just brought rain to the coast. For hundreds of years, merchants from elsewhere in Africa, Arabia, Persia, and India used the summer monsoon winds from the northeast to bring them south down the coast. They retraced their route in winter, returning with the southwest monsoon winds.

South of the equator steady westward-blowing winds also brought merchants to the coast, straight across the ocean from India. These winds were named trade winds by the crews of merchant sailing ships that used them to reach the African coast.

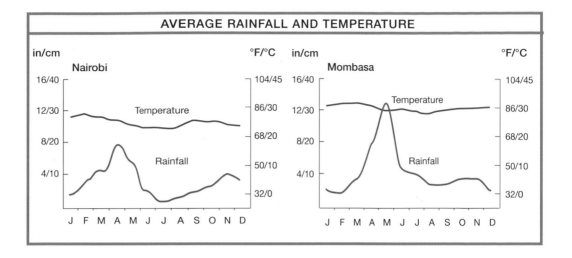

AVERAGE RAINFALL AND TEMPERATURE

Nairobi

in/cm — °F/°C

16/40 — 104/45
12/30 — 86/30
8/20 — 68/20
4/10 — 50/10
— 32/0

Temperature

Rainfall

J F M A M J J A S O N D

Mombasa

in/cm — °F/°C

16/40 — 104/45
12/30 — 86/30
8/20 — 68/20
4/10 — 50/10
— 32/0

Temperature

Rainfall

J F M A M J J A S O N D

Much like North America, the Central Highlands have four seasons. That is where the similarities end. From roughly January to March, the weather is sunny, dry, and warm. March to June is known as the time of the long rains; the short rains are from October to December. The period between the two rainy seasons (June to September) is cooler, cloudy, and dry.

The baobab tree, shown here, stores water in its trunk. In the background is Mount Kenya.

The western highlands have one long rainy season, while rain falls for only a few months each year on the grasslands. When rain comes, the land is transformed into green pastures grazed by many large wild animals. The extensive plains of the north, northeast, and some lower lands south of the Central Highlands have very little rain at all. The drier the land, the longer the dry season. When the torrential rains do come, dried-up riverbeds quickly flood and roads become impassable.

Lions are the most common of the big cats in Kenya. They generally hunt in groups, killing young, old, or sick animals. Attacks on humans are very rare.

WILDLIFE

Few other countries in the world have such a diverse range of animals, both large and small, as Kenya. The promise of seeing lions, zebras, giraffes, rhinos, and elephants in the wild draws thousands of tourists to Kenya each year. These animals are usually visible in the country's 40 parks and reserves, although the big cats are rarely seen. Most common are monkeys and baboons, which both can be a pest. Each environment—coast, savanna, mountain forest, and semidesert, for example—has its own particular mix of animals. Some animals, such as the elephant, range widely, living in almost any habitat that can sustain them. Antelopes, including several types of gazelle, are very successful grazers. There is generally at least one type of antelope in virtually all habitats, including both mountain and desert.

High Life

The dense forests of the central and western highlands conceal a great range of tree- and ground-living animals. Surprisingly, many animals of the grasslands also live in the forests: black-and-white colobus monkeys live in the canopy. Elephants graze and browse from the ground level up. Lions, with more hair and spots than the plains variety, hunt the abundant forest creatures, including waterbucks and the black-faced vervet monkey. Lions are lazy creatures and will often steal the prey of cheetahs or hyenas rather than bother to hunt them-

Secrets of the Sea

Coral reefs in the azure waters of the Indian Ocean are rich in marine life, from brightly-colored parrotfish to rare green turtles. Farther offshore are whales, dolphins, and many strange invertebrates (animals without a backbone). Reefs are built up of layer upon layer of the chalky skeletons of tiny animals called coral polyps, many of which live joined together in colonies that can be several feet wide. Only the top layer of a reef is living coral. Thousands of species of fish, including eels like the fearsome morays, as well as crabs, shrimps, worms, squid, octopus, shellfish, and rainbow-hued sea slugs find shelter and food on the reefs. Divers compare Kenya's animal-rich reefs to the world-famous reefs of the Red Sea and Australia's Great Barrier Reef.

Where they join with the sea, rivers and streams are often the location of vast mangrove (trees or shrubs) swamps. Among the very few flowering plants that can live in salty water, mangroves have dense networks of roots that prop the plants up. The swamps are home to a huge variety of fish, crabs, lobsters, shrimps, and shellfish. Many ocean-going fish and invertebrates spend their early years maturing in the relative safety of a mangrove swamp, away from fast predators of the open ocean like dolphins and sharks. Crocodiles sometimes lurk in the swamps, waiting to snap up passing frogs, small mammals, or turtles. Around Lamu gentle dugongs (a seal-like creature) graze underwater meadows of seagrass, although today only a few actually remain.

Fierce thunderstorms often rage over Lake Victoria and the surrounding lands. The Kisii Highlands in southwest Kenya have thunder 250 days a year!

selves. On the forest floor, warthogs, giant forest hogs, and bushpigs forage for food with their sensitive snouts. Bushpigs eat small frogs, mice, and worms as well as plants and fruits. One species of the red colobus monkey is unique to forests around the Tana River. Sykes' monkeys live above ground in the bamboo forests of Mount Kenya and the Aberdares. They eat plants and fruit and catch small birds and mammals. Crowned eagles snatch monkeys from the trees when they get hungry. Leopards occasionally drop from trees onto their prey but are much more likely to drag a fresh catch up a tree out of reach of scavengers. Some of these leopards have black coats—these are the legendary "black panthers."

Forest-dwelling antelopes include the tiny Kirk's dikdik and deerlike bushbucks. The rare mountain bongo, which lives on terrain at heights of up to 13,000 feet (4,000 m), is taller and heavier in Kenya than its relatives elsewhere. A striped coat helps conceal it in the forests. Several types of bird and other animals live only on the slopes of particular highlands, such as Mounts Elgon and Kenya and the Taita Hills.

Rock hyraxes live on cliffs and on the outcrops of rocks, which mainly occur in the highlands and mountains. These furry plant-eaters look a bit like rats but without the tail. Their cousins, the bush and tree hyraxes, live in the grasslands and forests of Kenya. Hyraxes are the favorite prey of Kenya's Verreaux eagles.

Kenyan Bird Life

Kenya's wide variety of habitat makes it a great area for birds. The country has the second-highest number of bird species in Africa (after the Democratic Republic of Congo), at more than 1,070 (North America has about 600), although only six are native to Kenya. Many birds found in Kenya are also commonly found in northern Europe but spend the winter in the country. Among the most numerous species native to Kenya are the colorful bee-eaters, of which there are 12 species, four of them quite common. Large walking birds include marabous and ostriches and flamingos which are found around the lakes. In the mountains and across the plains live six species of vulture, which travel great distances to feed.

Lake Life

Though surrounded by semidesert, Lakes Turkana and Baringo are as rich in wildlife as Lake Naivasha in the Central Highlands. Nile perch up to 6.5 feet (2 m) long, tigerfish, bichir, and various species of the popular food fish, tilapia, abound. Crocodiles and hippopotamuses slither or wade in the waters around the edge. Birds include African fish eagles and fish-eating cormorants, pelicans, and kingfishers. The soda lakes are home to flamingos, which come in matching shades of pink. Lake Naivasha is a popular weekend resort for Nairobi citizens.

Deserts and Semideserts

They might look barren, but dry lands are still home to a variety of animals perfectly adapted to life in the harsh conditions. The widespread Günther's dikdiks can live in dry, hot desert regions as long as there are a few plants, even wilted ones, such as aloes, euphorbias, and acacias to graze on. The upper lip of all dikdiks looks like the beginnings of an elephant's trunk. This is most obvious in Günther's dikdik. The long snout is used to control

Huge flocks of flamingos—sometimes up to a million—feed on the blue-green algae that form in the shallow waters of the soda lakes of the Rift Valley.

Kenya's Green Belt Movement, formed in 1977, has planted over 12 million trees across the country and has transformed environmental awareness.

temperature. To cool down, the dikdik pants through its nose to speed up heat loss. Gerbils store food and live underground, feeding at night to avoid the day's heat. Desert warthogs lack the sharp front teeth of their forest cousins and use their hard, sharp-edged lips to graze on the sandy floors. A few larger mammals live solitary lives in the dry lands, except when courting. Kudu antelopes with long spiral horns, up to 6.5 feet (2 m) long in some species, can survive without water on plants alone if the plants are juicy enough. Mulelike Grevy's zebras are hardy enough to live in scrubby grasslands with little rainfall.

Endangered Species

At least 30 species of animals are endangered in Kenya, and 18 are critically endangered. These animals, which include black rhinos, wild dogs, several types of monkeys, antelopes, birds, and the African elephant, are in danger of dying out completely if not protected. The loss of land to farming is one cause, but the numbers of larger animals are low after being hunted for many years. Elephants were killed for their tusks in the 1800s, when there was great demand for ivory in Europe. It was used to make piano keys, billiard balls, and ornaments. Big game safaris (hunts) were popular among Europeans who came to Kenya in the 1920s and 1930s in great numbers. U.S. novelist Ernest Hemingway acted out his fantasies of big game hunting while on safari in Kenya and Tanzania in 1933–1934. *The Green Hills of Africa* (1935) describes his adventures in what

is now Amboseli National Park. Kenya had all of the "big five" that were favorite game of sports hunters: lions, leopards, cheetahs, rhinos, and elephants. Leopards were popular for their coats, as was the Grevy's zebra, which was especially prized for its thin, evenly spaced stripes. Thousands of all these animals were killed by trophy hunters. More recently, rhinos have been targeted by hunters for their horns, which are used to make natural medicines in Asia. The horns are fashionable in Yemen as dagger handles.

Poaching has declined after laws were made that allow wardens to shoot poachers on sight. There have been conflicts with people who are no longer allowed to use the parkland, but more effort is now made to involve local people in managing and protecting the parks. This has motivated the people who live in the parks to prevent poaching.

Savannas

Large herds of grazing animals were once common to savannas all over the world. Now they remain only in Africa—in particular in the east African countries of Kenya and Tanzania. Buffalo, zebras, gnu (or wildebeest), rhinos, elephants, giraffes, and antelopes graze the tough grasses and herbs. Each animal prefers a different mix of plants, so they do not compete for food. Elephants and giraffes also browse on leaves and fruit from the thorny trees. Black rhinos prefer the edges of savannas and woodlands, but are only found in isolated pockets in southeastern Kenya and in the country's national parks.

Large herds of many different animals gather near water or where there is good pasture. Of the antelopes, bush duikers, gazelles, impalas, elands, hartebeest,

Elephants are found throughout Kenya's grasslands and forests. An adult elephant can eat up to 375 lb (170 kg) of plant material a day but they are essential to the ecology of certain areas.

Cheetahs are expert hunters. Aided by excellent eyesight and long legs, they can reach short bursts of speed of up to 70 mph (100 kph).

and the cattlelike gnu are common. Somali galagos, a type of bushbaby, are happy to live in thornbushes in woods and grassland thickets, descending to ground-level to catch insects.

Kenya is one of the last places on earth where the fastest land animals—cheetahs—might still be glimpsed rushing their prey, but few remain. Lions and wild dogs work in groups of their own kind to stalk the grazers and browsers, such as gazelles and other antelopes. Leopards hunt alone, relying on their speed and excellent camouflage. Hyenas have powerful jaws and shoulders for carrying carcasses with, and they are equipped to chew and digest bones and teeth. They not only eat animals killed by others, but are capable hunters themselves. Servals are wildcats that prey on small rodents like the crested porcupine or ground squirrels as well as birds and antelopes.

In so-called termite savannas, termite mounds provide floodproof sites where trees and shrubs can grow. The aardwolf, cousin to the hyena, laps up the termites with its long tongue. Scaly anteaters (or pangolins) are animals with both fur and armor plating that live wherever termites live.

PLANT LIFE

Kenya's different terrains mean that it has an equally diverse range of plant life. The most common image of the country is perhaps that of the endless plain. Plains exist in the far south of the country, with their baobab trees, and whistling thornbushes. The south is also home to fast-growing grasses, which are trampled by herds of animals. Such landscapes also exist in the arid north, although here there are more scaly-barked species such as the acacia and euphorbia, and the ground is often bare.

The lower slopes of Mounts Kenya and Eglon, the Mau Escarpment, and the Aberdares are home to evergreen temperate forest. Above 6,500 feet (2,000 m) lies open marshy moorland, home to groundsel trees and giant lobelias. Mount Kenya also supports an Afro-Alpine plant life that is found on other east African mountains, low-growing alpine plants, and heather.

West of the Rift Valley near Lake Victoria is the Kakamega, an equatorial forest more characteristic of the thick forests of central and west Africa. There is very little lowland rain forest in Kenya, although some remains around the Athi and Tana Rivers. Kenya's coasts have mangrove swamps which are farmed. Termite-proof mangrove timber is exported to the Middle East.

The giant lobelia is found on the upper slopes of Mount Kenya and the country's other uplands.

Kenya's National Parks

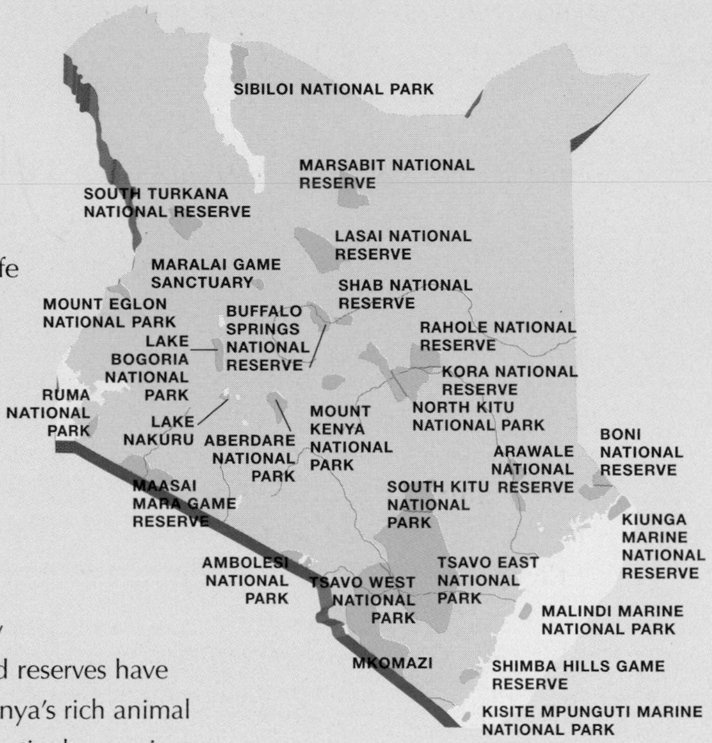

Kenya has 43 national parks and reserves covering more than 7.6 percent of the country's land. There are also three marine parks. National parks are run by the Kenyan Wildlife Service (KWS); reserves are run by local authorities but the staff works for the KWS. The parks are as diverse as the land is, including the glaciers of Mount Kenya, savannas, forests, and dry scrublands. The parks and reserves have been set up to protect Kenya's rich animal life, sometimes for one particular species that is declining. Arawale Reserve was created in 1973 to protect the rare Hunter's antelope, for instance. Arid Sibiloi National Park was set up to protect the prehistoric site of Koobi Fora. It also has plenty of wildlife, from rare Grevy's zebras to more than 12,000 Nile crocodiles in Lake Turkana. Lakes Nakuru and Bogoria national parks are famous for their spectacular bird life. Lake Nakuru is said to have more flamingos per square foot than anywhere else in the world, with at least a million in total. It is also famous for waterbucks. These small antelopes never stray far from a source of

water. They need to drink large amounts to help digest the tough plants they eat. Around the shores of Lake Nakuru hundreds of male waterbucks defend territories of up to 100 acres (40 hectares) each.

Maasai Mara National Park is perhaps the most famous. As the grasses recede with the seasons, thousands of people travel to Kenya to see the annual migration of huge herds of animals, including thousands of wildebeest in the Maasai Mara. Tsavo East and Tsavo West are the two largest national parks.

The map labels include:

- SIBILOI NATIONAL PARK
- MARSABIT NATIONAL RESERVE
- SOUTH TURKANA NATIONAL RESERVE
- LASAI NATIONAL RESERVE
- MARALAI GAME SANCTUARY
- SHAB NATIONAL RESERVE
- MOUNT EGLON NATIONAL PARK
- BUFFALO SPRINGS NATIONAL RESERVE
- RAHOLE NATIONAL RESERVE
- LAKE BOGORIA NATIONAL PARK
- KORA NATIONAL RESERVE
- RUMA NATIONAL PARK
- LAKE NAKURU
- MOUNT KENYA NATIONAL PARK
- NORTH KITU NATIONAL PARK
- BONI NATIONAL RESERVE
- ABERDARE NATIONAL PARK
- ARAWALE NATIONAL RESERVE
- MAASAI MARA GAME RESERVE
- SOUTH KITU NATIONAL PARK
- KIUNGA MARINE NATIONAL RESERVE
- AMBOLESI NATIONAL PARK
- TSAVO WEST NATIONAL PARK
- TSAVO EAST NATIONAL PARK
- MALINDI MARINE NATIONAL PARK
- MKOMAZI
- SHIMBA HILLS GAME RESERVE
- KISITE MPUNGUTI MARINE NATIONAL PARK

CITIES

Today around 28 percent of Kenya's population live in towns and cities. The figure is growing fast, though, as Kenya becomes more and more urbanized each year. Unlike western Africa, which had a long history of urbanization before the arrival of Europeans, Kenya had virtually no large urban settlements before it became a British colony, except along the coast. Towns and ports such as Lamu, Malindi, and Mombasa are among the oldest urban settlements in the country. Today, the interior of Kenya also has several important urban areas, including Nairobi, Kisumu, Nakuru, and Eldoret.

City of the Sun

Its residents call Nairobi the City of the Sun. It is a place of international importance. To the United Nations, Nairobi is its fourth "World Center." The city is headquarters of the UN Environment Program and is also

Nairobi's skyline is crowded with the skyscrapers of international business.

east Africa's trade hub. Jomo Kenyatta Airport, a 25-minute drive from town, is one of the busiest international airports in Africa, handling up to 4 million arrivals a year. Recently, two international-size stadiums were built: the Nyayo Stadium and the Moi International Sports Complex. The population is equally international, and Nairobi is a truly multicultural city, with both visitors and residents from other parts of Africa, Europe, Asia, and the Americas. This is reflected in the city's huge range of eateries, including French, Swahili, Thai, Ethiopian, Japanese, Greek, Indian, and Italian. The city is always lively, especially at night. Yet this modern, cosmopolitan city has been built on what little more than 100 years ago was a barren, bleak, and swampy site.

> The land on which Nairobi was founded is at the junction of Kikuyu, Maasai, and Kamba territories. Nairobi comes from the Maasai's name for the land: *enkare nyarobi*, "the place of cold, or sweet, waters."

About Town

The heart of Nairobi is the well-planned commercial center, with its neat, gridlike arrangement of streets. The influence of India can be seen in the city center's older buildings, but today the streets include many high-rise office buildings of steel and glass. Kenyatta Avenue is a four-lane-wide route that cuts right through the commercial center. It was originally designed to be wide enough to allow a team of 12 oxen to do a full turn. Moi Avenue, a slightly smaller but just as important road, cuts across the northeastern end of Kenyatta Avenue. These avenues divide the city center into three sections. The southwest division, based around City Square, is where government buildings and high-rise office buildings are found. Luxury hotels and upmarket shops flourish in this wealthy part of the

Laborers being driven to work along Kenyatta Avenue.

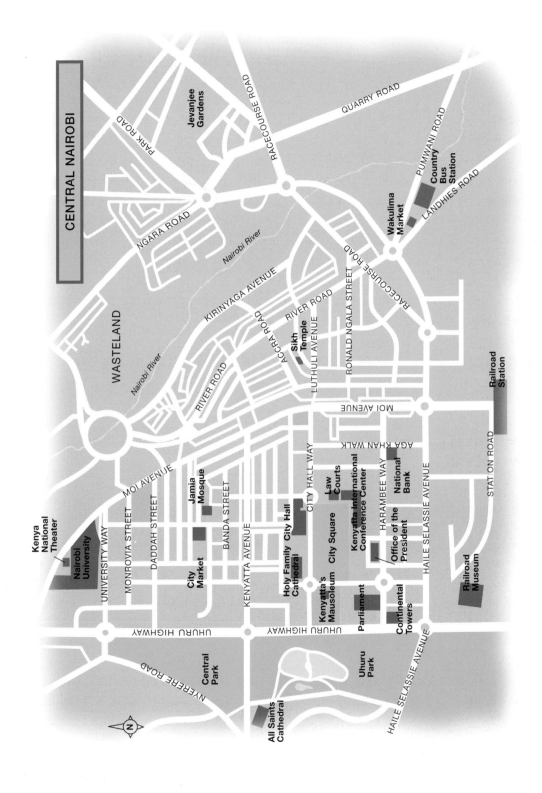

CENTRAL NAIROBI

Jevanjee Gardens

PARK ROAD

RACECOURSE ROAD

QUARRY ROAD

PUMWANI ROAD

Country Bus Station

LANDHIES ROAD

Wakulima Market

NGARA ROAD

Nairobi River

KIRINYAGA AVENUE

RACECOURSE ROAD

WASTELAND

Nairobi River

ACCRA ROAD

RIVER ROAD

Sikh Temple

RIVER ROAD

LUTHULI AVENUE

RONALD NGALA STREET

Railroad Station

MOI AVENUE

AGA KHAN WALK

STATION ROAD

MOI AVENUE

CITY HALL WAY

Law Courts

Kenyatta International Conference Center

HARAMBEE WAY

National Bank

HAILE SELASSIE AVENUE

Jamia Mosque

BANDA STREET

Kenya National Theater

Nairobi University

UNIVERSITY WAY

MONROVIA STREET

DADDAH STREET

City Market

KENYATTA AVENUE

Holy Family Cathedral

City Hall

City Square

Office of the President

Railroad Museum

Kenyatta's Mausoleum

Parliament

Continental Towers

UHURU HIGHWAY

UHURU HIGHWAY

HAILE SELASSIE AVENUE

NYERERE ROAD

Central Park

Uhuru Park

All Saints Cathedral

HAILE SELASSIE AVENUE

N

The "Lunatic Line"

On May 30, 1896, the first section of track was laid of a railroad that would stretch from Mombasa to the shores of Lake Victoria more than 300 miles (480 km) away. The British wanted a railroad to improve access to Uganda, which had become one of their colonies in 1893. Those British who opposed the building of the expensive railroad dubbed it the "lunatic line," because they thought it was a waste of money. Nairobi was founded as a supply base before the hazardous ascent into the highlands began. The site was used as a shunting yard for trains, administrative center, and camping ground by the nearly 3,000 Africans, around 30,000 Indians, and the few European officials working on the railroad.

No one knew then that Nairobi would one day become the capital city of Kenya. At that time, "Kenya" as a distinct nation did not exist. In 1895, however, the British claimed what is now Kenya as part of their British East Africa protectorate (colony). Before the railroad was completed, European settlers were being encouraged to emigrate to the fertile highlands of central Kenya. The Kikuyu people were pushed off their land and restricted to cramped reserves with poor soils. With the arrival of more and more Europeans, Nairobi grew even larger. With no land to farm and forced by taxes into paid work, many Kikuyu migrated to the city in hope of finding jobs in the factories.

Despite the exploitative nature of the original building scheme, the "lunatic line" is one of the world's great railroads and has been of huge economic importance for the region. In 1907, Nairobi became the capital of British East Africa. As its importance grew, more people flocked to the city from rural areas. When Kenya became independent in 1963, Nairobi remained the capital.

Nairobi boasts more shopping malls than any African city outside South Africa.

city. City Square itself is a flagstoned court flanked on one side by a statue of Jomo Kenyatta, Kenya's first president, which stands in front of the parliament buildings, and on the other by Kenyatta's mausoleum, which is permanently lit by torchlight. The imposing Roman Catholic Holy Family Cathedral and the towering Kenyatta International Conference Center, with its revolving roof-top restaurant, also overlook the square.

At the southernmost end of Moi Avenue is the train station, still at the heart of the city. Next door is the

Railroad Museum, with its carefully restored steam engines. The history of the "Lunatic Line" (*see* box opposite) is vividly described inside. A railroad car from which one British official was dragged and hauled by a man-eating lion is on display.

North of Kenyatta Avenue, stores, restaurants, and hotels still flourish, such as those in City Market, but most are smaller and more affordable than the ones farther south. It is the city's main shopping center for food, clothes, arts, and crafts. Kiondo baskets made from woven sisal (a strong cord fiber made from agave) and the famous Kisii soapstone carvings are sold in the markets. Nairobi's main mosque is in this district, the elaborately decorated green-and-white Jamia Mosque. Jevanjee Gardens, off Moi Avenue, were designed by the man they are named after in the early 1900s. A.M. Jevanjee was a leading Indian Nairobi businessman, campaigner for racial equality, and founder of the

Uhuru (Freedom) Park in the center of Nairobi is overlooked by the buildings of the city's administrative quarter.

Urban Pioneers

Indian East Africans played important roles, as traders, merchants, and shopkeepers in the development of Kenya's towns and cities, especially Nairobi. After the railroad was built, Indians were among the first to bring commercial and manufactured goods to areas far from the railroad. Though most returned home, some of the Indian laborers who worked on the railroad stayed on in Kenya. They were joined by others who came to set up trading outposts. Asians were not allowed to buy land, so they were forced to stay in urban areas. In 1900, the first Indian bazaar was opened in Nairobi, and the city soon became a trading center as well as a supply town.

Standard newspaper. His building work did much to shape the look of Nairobi. In the northerly part of Nairobi city is the university district and the Kenya National Theater. The building of the National Museum lies even farther north, on the edge of the city. It houses fascinating collections about Kenya's history, from the earliest known human ancestors to modern-day peoples and their unique cultures, as well as modern art collections from Kenya and Uganda and an extensive collection of birds.

East of Moi Avenue lies Nairobi's poorer inner-city region, known as the River Road district. This part of the city is least popular with tourists, though a few luxury hotels have recently been

Kibera shantytown lies to the southwest of central Nairobi, close to the wealthier district of the Ngong Hills.

Parks in the City

Nairobi is a green city. Besides tree-lined avenues, it has Central Park and Uhuru ("Freedom") Park, which are both within the city center. The largest green space, City Park, lies to the north of the center, and the Arboretum, which is fairly overgrown, lies to the west. Packed with hundreds of species of tropical trees and plants, the larger parks are also home to colorful birds and the odd group of monkeys. Nairobi citizens defend these parks vigorously against developers who try to build upon lands within their borders. Most impressive of all is Nairobi National Park, less than a 20-minute drive south from the city center. Inside the park, visitors can see lions, impalas, giraffes, leopards, wildebeest, and buffalo against the unusual backdrop of Nairobi's skyscrapers. The park is an important sanctuary for rhinos, but there are no elephants living there. Hippos and crocodiles swim in the Athi River, which runs to the east of the park.

built. While not a slum, the River Road district is densely populated and bustling with activity. Its Sikh temple, like many others, offers free food and a bed for the night to visitors. The Nairobi River borders the district on the northeast side, and a strip of wasteland separates it from the suburbs. The busy eastern suburb of Eastleigh is home to many Somalis, and has earned the nickname of "Little Mogadishu" (Mogadishu is the capital of Somalia) from the other citizens of Nairobi.

The Maasai say that the Ngong Hills east of Nairobi were formed by a giant tripping over Mt. Kilimanjaro and hitting his head on the ground.

Although author Karen Blixen's house has been restored, the set of Nairobi used in the film Out of Africa *and built nearby was demolished after shooting.*

Around Town

Thousands of acres of suburbs surround the commercial heart of Nairobi. Those to the east and south are increasingly poor, some with hastily constructed flimsy housing and limited facilities. The majority of homes do not have running water or electricity, relying on the polluted waters of the Nairobi River for drinking and washing. These so-called shantytowns, including Mathare Valley, Kibera, and Korogocho, house the steady trickle of migrants to the city. People come into Nairobi from the surrounding rural areas in search of employment and somewhere to live.

The wealthy Karen district and the Ngong Hills on the outskirts of southwest Nairobi remind visitors of Kenya's colonial days; many Europeans still live there today. Ngong's most famous resident was Karen Blixen, the Danish author of *Out of Africa*, which she published under the pen name Isak Dinesen. The famous 1985 Hollywood film based on her book starring Robert Redford and Meryl Streep was filmed in Nairobi Province. Blixen's farmhouse (*see above*) was presented to Kenya on its independence by the Danish government. It has been thoroughly restored and is now a museum.

Harry Thuku

Nairobi's Harry Thuku Road is named after Kenya's first nationalist leader. The movement he led protested against the dominance of white settlers in the colonial government in the early 20th century. Thuku was arrested in 1922 and exiled for seven years. In protest, what was probably Kenya's first serious political demonstration was staged outside Nairobi's central police station in March 1922. More than 20 of the demonstrators were shot dead.

Mombasa

Mombasa probably existed as an African settlement before the arrival of Arab merchants who are often credited with its foundation. The city has long been one of east Africa's chief centers, even before Kenya existed, and is now the main port in the region. It has one of the best natural harbors on the whole coast. This beachless tropical island nestles in its own snugly-fitting coastal bay and measures just 5.5 square miles (14 sq. km). The island is linked by bridge, causeway, and ferry to a much larger urban area on the mainland, bringing the total size of Mombasa to 100 square miles (260 sq. km).

Mombasa has two ports, one old and one new. Old Port is on the island's east side. Small craftlike dhows use this port en route to Africa, Arabia, or India. Trade in rubber, sisal, cloves, and cowrie shells made Mombasa rich and powerful in the past. The dhows did not have engines, and they came from as far away as Arabia, Persia (modern Iran), and India. Many Indians settled in the city and today it has a large Asian population. Kilindini, a modern deep-water port, lies on the west side of the island.

Mombasa's Old Town has a mixture of architectural styles, including the traditional Swahili style (see pp.102–103), 19th-century Indian styles, and British colonial buildings.

Nairobi, the capital, is Kenya's largest urban area with about 1.5 million residents. Mombasa, the main port, is the next largest with a population of around 500,000.

Sisal, cotton, sugar, and agricultural products are shipped out from Kilindini. Sent from Tanzania, Rwanda, Burundi, the Democratic Republic of Congo (Zaire), Sudan, and Uganda, goods leave Mombasa for Europe, America, Asia, and the Middle East.

At different times in its history, Mombasa was controlled by Swahili people, Arabs, Portuguese, Zanzibaris, and the British. The British made Mombasa the capital of their British East Africa protectorate, or colony, in 1887. It remained the capital until replaced by Nairobi in 1907.

Fort Jesus

Overlooking the Old Port is Mombasa's most famous sight: Fort Jesus. One of the best examples of 16th-century military architecture to protect their trading activities, building by the Portuguese began in 1593, and took five years to complete. Since then, it has changed hands many times as Omani Arabs repeatedly wrested power from the Portuguese. For the first half of the 20th century it was used as a prison by the British (until 1958). Today, it is a museum and national park, with exhibits on Swahili life and culture. Ancient Chinese pottery once traded along the coast and items brought up from a sunken Portuguese warship are on display. The frigate *Santo Antonio de Tanna* was sunk more than 300 years ago off Mombasa by Omani Arabs. It was excavated in the 1970s by a joint Kenyan–International team.

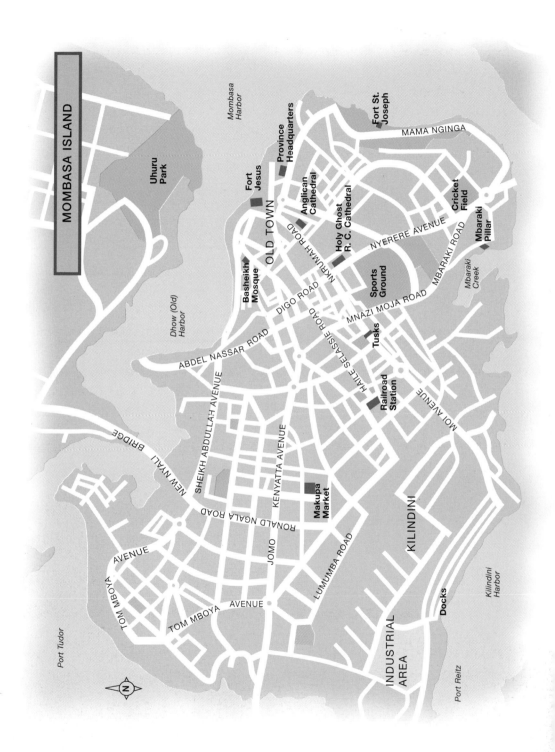

MOMBASA ISLAND

Mombasa Harbor

Uhuru Park

Fort St. Joseph

MAMA NGINGA

Province Headquarters

Fort Jesus

OLD TOWN

Anglican Cathedral

Holy Ghost R. C. Cathedral

Cricket Field

Mbaraki Pillar

NYERERE AVENUE

MBARAKI ROAD

Mbaraki Creek

Basheikh Mosque

NKRUMAH ROAD

DIGO ROAD

Sports Ground

MNAZI MOJA ROAD

Dhow (Old) Harbor

ABDEL NASSAR ROAD

HAILE SELASSIE ROAD

Tusks

Railroad Station

MOI AVENUE

SHEIKH ABDULLAH AVENUE

KENYATTA AVENUE

NEW NYALI BRIDGE

RONALD NGALA ROAD

Makupa Market

JOMO

LUMUMBA ROAD

KILINDINI

AVENUE

TOM MBOYA

TOM MBOYA AVENUE

INDUSTRIAL AREA

Docks

Kilindini Harbor

Port Tudor

Port Reitz

N

Mombasa's harbor, next to the Old Town on the eastern side of the island, was the site of the first settlement.

Old and New Mombasa

Few of the houses in Mombasa's Old Town are more than a century old, yet this eastern district harks back in its architecture to how the Swahili towns must have looked centuries ago. There is still a mix of African and Arabic influences, as well as 19th-century colonial and Indian styles. The narrow winding streets slope toward the Old Port and are overlooked by houses one or two stories high. Homes feature intricately carved Swahili doors and Arabic-style balconies with elaborate lattice-work. The magnificent Burhani Mosque, near Old Port, contrasts with the older-style buildings. This is just one of the more than 50 mosques and dozens of Hindu and Sikh temples on the island. The Jain temple on the edge of the Old Town is a beautifully ornate building.

Surrounding the Old Town is modern Mombasa, with its wide streets and a small but increasing number of high-rise buildings. This area is relatively undeveloped considering the size of its population and until recently there was only one working set of traffic lights. The water supply in Mombasa is still fairly unreliable, a problem in a city that has a steamy, humid climate. The town center is the crossroads of Moi Avenue with

The fine lattice-work screens and railings found on some of Mombasa's older buildings were a feature that shielded the Muslim women who lived there from the eyes of passersby.

Nyerere, Nkrumah, and Digo roads. Nearby, a pair of crossed aluminum elephant tusks point skyward on either side of Moi Avenue. They were put up in honor of the coronation of Britain's Queen Elizabeth II in 1953. Stalls line the sides of Moi Avenue, selling goods like sisal baskets, soapstone and wood carvings, and fabrics. Majengo is an area of low-income housing located around Makupa Market at the heart of the western half of the island. The southwest corner of the island is given over to industry. On the mainland, Changamwe and Likoni are fast-growing but neglected suburbs. Mombasa Airport brings visitors to the mainland west of the island. Along the coast north of the city is a series of fine beaches and the Bamburi National Quarry Park, a wildlife reserve that has been formed from a reclaimed stone quarry.

Unlike Nairobi, which is called by some Nairobbery because of its high crime rate, Mombasa is quite safe as a city, even after dark. As a result, many shops and bars stay open late into the night.

An overview of the city of Kisumu. To the left is Lake Victoria.

Kisumu

Lying on the shores of Lake Victoria in the far west of Kenya, Kisumu is the country's third-largest city and the capital of Nyanza (Lake) Province. Its prosperity has traditionally been based on trade across the lake with Uganda and Tanzania. The city was linked to Uganda by steamship in 1895 and then to Mombasa by train in 1903. By the height of British colonialism in the 1930s, Kisumu had become a major trade and transportation center for east Africa, supported by investments from Indian businesses, which had developed after the building of the railroad. With the break up of the East Africa Community in 1977, however, and the resultant fall in trade, the city went into a decline from which it has never fully recovered. The city's main street is Oginga Odinga Road, along which lie most of the city's shops and banks. The other central street is Jomo Kenyatta Avenue, home to the more expensive hotels, to the north it becomes the Kenyatta Highway.

The city slopes gently toward Lake Victoria, the distinctive smell of which pervades the city. Lower-

Lake Victoria

Only a small fraction of this vast freshwater lake—the second-largest in the world after Lake Superior—lies within Kenya's borders. By far the majority of the lake lies in Uganda and Tanzania. It covers 27,020 sq. miles (70,000 sq. km) and for 500 years its shores were settled by the Luo people. They called the lake Ukerewe. Europeans in the 19th century established that the lake was the source of the Nile. Today Lake Victoria faces problems from the water hyacinth, whose rapid growth chokes much of its waters.

lying than the capital Nairobi, Kisumu is hot and the lake creates very high humidity, which can be overwhelming. Much of the port area, including the city's warehouses and dockworker houses, are still run-down. However, trade between Kenya, Tanzania, and Uganda picked up in the late 1990s, although it still has a long way to go before it reaches earlier levels. The partial rebuilding of the earlier trade community, combined with the recent routing of the UN World Food Program through the port to help the war-torn states of Rwanda, Burundi, Uganda, and Congo, have revived activity in Kisumu. However, there is a greater problem with infrastructure: 60 percent of the population of the city live without a fresh source of water, cholera is a constant threat, and garbage collection is not reliable. Kisumu now suffers continual unemployment and as a result many of those citizens, who are able to, have migrated elsewhere. Despite these problems, Kisumu is an attractive city, with its central position on Lake Victoria offering it the hope of future development.

Kisumu's oldest quarter lies to the east on the shores of Lake Victoria, while the more modern, industrial district lies farther inland.

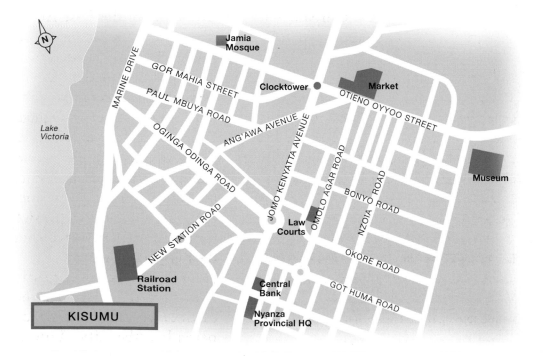

Past and Present

"How we look at yesterday has important bearings on how we look at today and how we see the possibilities of tomorrow."

Kenyan novelist, critic, and playwright Ngugi wa Thiong'o

Nearly the whole history of the human race can be traced in Kenya, starting with some of our earliest human ancestors. Few written records exist to tell us about Kenya's less distant past, yet much of the country's history is known. It has been passed down from generation to generation in stories, songs, and ceremonies and has been backed up by scientific studies of languages, cultures, artifacts, and settlements.

There are records of Arab trading along the coast of East Africa as far back as the seventh century, accounts borne out by the obvious Islamic influence upon the culture of the coastal region. Later, in the 16th century, the Portuguese established trading bases along the coast.

Portuguese colonialists were forced out by Omanis at the end of the 17th century and they in turn by the British in the following century. The attempts of the British to carve up large areas of East Africa for their own economic gain led to the building of a large administrative system, a railroad, and links between eastern and western Kenya. The self-serving nature of British rule and encouragement of white settlement starting in the late 19th century led to calls for independence in the early 20th century. Independence was finally achieved in 1963. Since then Kenya has made strides to build itself into a modern democracy. Today its central role in east African trade makes it an important presence in the region.

The ruins of Gedi, a 13th-century Arab-Swahili town abandoned in the 17th century, are one of the main historical monuments on the Kenyan coast.

FACT FILE

• Kenya's role in African history as a major migratory route is shown by the fact that today the country is home to almost every major African language group.

• The Kenyan interior, which was occupied by Maasai animal herders, remained safe from outsiders until the 1880s.

• Nairobi replaced Mombasa as the capital of Kenya in 1907.

• In 1920 there were 9,000 white settlers living in Kenya, but by the 1950s, with the offer of land to white settlers at rock-bottom prices, the figure had reached 80,000.

HOMINID REMAINS IN EAST AFRICA

The map shows the main hominid finds in eastern Africa, largely clustered around the Rift Valley and the nearby lakes.

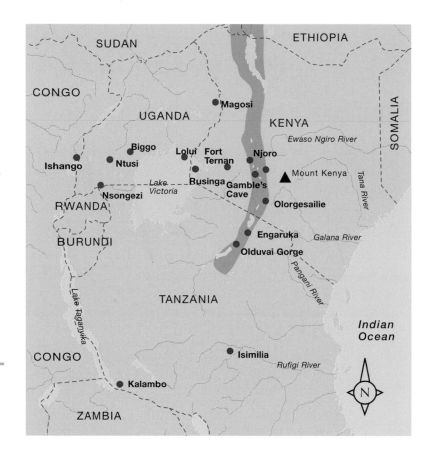

KEY

● Hominid remains

▮ Rift Valley

THE CRADLE OF HUMANITY?

Over many millions of years, apelike creatures who walked earth upright on two legs developed into modern humans. In many parts of Kenya, scientists have found the preserved remains (fossils) of these apelike creatures, some more distant relations than direct human ancestors. Because the fossils of these ancient hominids are older than any found elsewhere, east Africa has earned the nickname "the cradle of humanity." Some scientists even suggest that the formation of the Rift Valley, a vast upheaval that massively changed the region's ecology, may have been the event that caused the human species to evolve from its earlier ancestors.

One group of scientists central to the discovery of hominid remains in east Africa has been the Leakey family. The English-born Kenyan husband-and-wife team, Mary (1913–1996) and Louis Leakey (1903–1972), discovered fragments of a 1.75-million-year-old skull in Olduvai Gorge, just south of the Kenya–Tanzania border in 1959. Their son Richard Leakey (born 1944), his wife, Maeve, and their Kenyan coworkers Kamoya Kimeu and Bernard Ngeves discovered even older fossils, 4.2 million years old, around the shores of Lake Turkana in northern Kenya. Kimeu, the leader of the sharp-eyed "Hominid Gang," made some of the most important finds, including the near complete 1.6-million-year-old skeleton of Nariokotome boy (*see* box below) in 1984. Maeve Leakey said of Kimeu: "No one can find them like Kimeu can." The precise development of the human species from its more primitive hominid ancestors is still being researched.

At Olorgesailie, south of Nairobi, thousands of hand axes dating from 900,000 to 600,000 years ago can be seen spilling out of the earth. Why so many tools were left in this prehistoric site is a mystery. It may have been a storage place for a community's tools.

Nariokotome Boy

The boy that Kimeu unearthed on the western shores of Lake Turkana in northern Kenya would have been surprisingly tall and upright when he was alive. He was well fed on a diet of fish, fruits, honey, seeds, and meat. Archaeologists can tell this from the remains of seeds and bones found near his body. As an adult, he would have grown to more than 6 feet (1.8 m) tall. He would have lived with a small group of people, who hunted, fished, and gathered food together in the region. Some of his people might have had the job of making tools; others would have had the task of collecting the stones to make into tools. The animals they hunted could have included short-necked giraffes, huge elephants, and baboons up to twice the size of their modern relatives. Saber-tooth tigers, giant crocodiles, and other predators were scared off with fire—these early humans probably struck flint tools together to make sparks. Tough roots of plants might have been thrown onto the fires for softening, leading to the invention of cooking. We can tell from archaeological evidence that the Nariokotome boy died from blood poisoning after one of his baby teeth fell out and his gums became infected.

THE PEOPLING OF KENYA

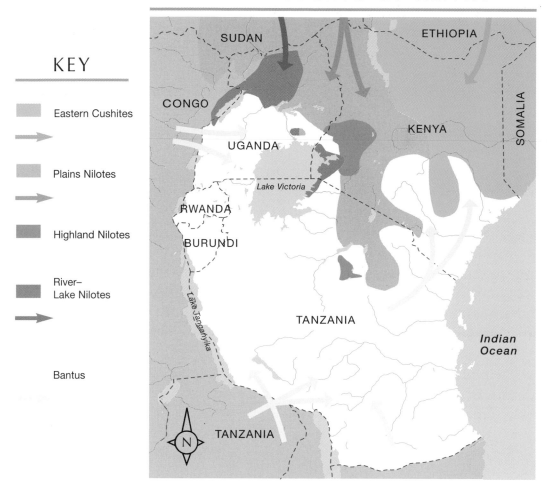

KEY

Eastern Cushites

Plains Nilotes

Highland Nilotes

River–
Lake Nilotes

Bantus

This map shows the first peoples to settle in the region now occupied by Kenya and its neighbors. The Nilotes and Cushites came from the north, while Bantus came from western Africa.

THE PEOPLING OF KENYA

Most Kenyans are descended from one or more of three main groups of Africans: the Cushites, Nilotes, and Bantus. These are not distinct "tribes" but people who speak the same or related languages. Through intermarriage, trade, and conquest they have given rise to most of the many ethnic groups that live in Kenya today. A fourth group, hunter-gatherers distinctive for their short stature and languages that use click sounds, lived in East Africa long before the arrival of the Cushites, Bantus, and Nilotes. The women gathered fruits, seeds, and edible plants and the men hunted game to survive.

No direct descendants of these people remain in Kenya today. Elements of their culture have lived on among the Okiek (or Dorobo) of the highlands, the Sanye of the Tana River, and a few other groups.

The peopling of the region was a slow process, occurring gradually over many centuries and starting more than 3,000 years ago. Famine, drought, population growth, conquest, and the need to escape harsh rulers might have forced the ancient migrants to move on. Traveling in small groups, or just family by family, they moved from one settlement to the next.

Cushites

Cushitic people were the first to arrive in Kenya. Throughout the second millennium B.C. (2000–1000 B.C.), they migrated south from the Ethiopian Highlands, which sit just beyond the northern border of modern Kenya. Cushites share ancestors with the Arabs, western Asians, and Europeans. They were the first farmers of the area, growing cereal crops such as millet and sorghum. Although they spread throughout the whole of what is now Kenya, in the south no distinct Cushitic groups remain. The Cushites were absorbed by Nilotic and Bantu peoples who arrived in the area after them. Direct descendants live only in the dry northern regions of Kenya, namely the Oromo (or Galla), the Rendille, and the Somali peoples. Many are descended from more recent migrants from the Ethiopian Highlands in about the 14th century A.D. and later.

The fossil hominids in Kenya are among the most abundant in the world. The bones of more than 150 hominids, ranging from 1.5 to 2 million years old have been found at Koobi Fora, Lake Turkana, alone. They are housed in the National Museum of Kenya, Nairobi, in a bomb-proof vault.

The Central Rift

The Central Rift is home to an important site that was probably inhabited by Cushitic peoples about 3,000 years ago: Hyrax Hill. Graves lined with stone and covered by flat stone lids contained the remains of men and women buried with their possessions. The many finds included obsidian tools, pottery, and grinding stones. Obsidian is a glassy black, brown, or red stone formed when lava cools quickly.

The Great Rift Valley has long been used like a giant highway by humans, and even earlier by other hominids, moving in and out of East Africa. Rivers flowing from the valley to the sea, such as the Athi/Galana River, were a well-used route to and from the coast.

Besides English and Swahili, Kenya's two official languages, there are a number of major languages spoken in the country today, including Kikuyu, Luo, Kikamba, Maasai, and Samburu. In addition there are numerous other minor languages.

Although originally a farming people, the Oromo, Rendille, and Somalis are now more likely to be herders of cattle, goats, camels, and sheep.

Nilotes

After the Cushites came the Nilotes, who are named for the area they originally came from—the Nile River region of southern Sudan, to the southwest of the Ethiopian Highlands. They are divided into three groups according to the area they migrated into. From about 1000 B.C. to 1500 A.D., the Highland and Plains Nilotes migrated into the highlands and plains of Kenya. The Highland Nilotes were the first to arrive, and by the 1600s they occupied the fertile highlands. Today, the descendants of these settlers are called Kalenjin, but the various groups only acquired this name in the late 20th century. A radio commentator with this ancestry became famous for his catchphrase:

The Kalenjin

The Kalenjin are the largest group of the Highland Nilotes who migrated into east Africa during the first millennium B.C., where they mixed with Bantu peoples from the south and west. They are some of the earliest inhabitants of Kenya and may have absorbed earlier groups such as the hunter-gatherers of the forest and grasslands distinctive for their short stature.

Some Kalenjin were animal herders and looked down on those people who relied on cultivation for their food. They migrated south from southern Sudan as the climate changed and the northern forests declined, first settling in the area to the west of Lake Turkana. Some

Kalenjin groups retained their hunter-gatherer existence, while others became agriculturalists, involved in beekeeping, and using honey in trading and for brewing beer.

Historically the Kalenjin were ruled by a *kok*, an informal gathering of the clan's elders. After adolescence men were divided into groups differentiated by age.

After 1978 the Kalenjin became very important in Kenyan politics, many of them given positions by Kenya's president Daniel arap Moi—himself a Kalenjin from Eldoret. Opponents have accused Moi of failing to prevent attacks on the Kikuyu in the Rift Valley villages.

"I tell you!" ("*Kalenjin!*"). People came to identify this term with anyone who spoke the same language as the commentator, and it is now the accepted name for Kenya's Highland Nilotes. Kalenjin-speaking people include the Pokot, Kipsigis, Okiek, and Nandi. Nilotic peoples were usually animal herders. The majority of Highland Nilotes still herd animals but there are many groups that only farm, as well as some who both farm and herd.

Plains Nilotes are responsible for the modern-day Maasai, Turkana, Iteso, and Samburu populations, who are also mostly herders of goats, cattle, and sheep, and camels in the north of Kenya. The Maasai were the most recent arrivals.

The third Nilotic group are the River-Lake Nilotes, who continued farther south

than other groups. They settled around the rivers and lakes of east-central Africa. The only Kenyan people of River-Lake Nilote descent, the Luo, live in the west of the country. The first Luo speakers probably arrived in what is now Nyanza Province in the 1500s. Other Luo arrived much later in the 17th century, including one group led by their king, Owiny Sigoma. He was known as a great conqueror. The Luo had wars among themselves and with their neighbors, the Maasai and Nandi. They were an adaptable people, however, who,

This Luo elder, from Kisumu in western Kenya, wears a headdress of ostrich feathers and hippo tusks.

although originally pastoralists (animal herders), soon took to farming the fertile soils and fishing the great lake. Cattle remained important to them, though, and a person would not be considered rich unless he owned a few cows.

Bantu Speakers

More than 2,000 years ago in the dense forests between west Africa's two mighty rivers, the Niger and the Congo, lived the ancestors of the modern-day Bantu-speakers. Over the next 2,000 years they dispersed from this region, at first keeping to the belt of rain forest across the middle of Africa but by 500 B.C. moving into the grasslands of eastern and southern Africa. By the early centuries of the first millennium A.D. they had already reached what is now the Kenyan coast and begun to move northward along it. The Bantu brought with them iron-working skills, which they used to make farming tools. Having knives to clear forest with and hoes to farm with, people were able to work more efficiently. Larger, more stable settlements developed as a result. Today Bantu peoples account for the vast majority of Africans. In Kenya, the largest Bantu groups are the Kisii, Meru, Kamba, and Kikuyu of the southwest and center, and the coastal Mijikenda people. Most Bantu-speaking peoples are farmers, often growing a variety of crops for their own food and to sell. The word Bantu is an invention of 20th-century linguists and comes from the stem *ntu*, meaning "person" and the plural prefix *ba*.

Kwale District, next to the coast just south of Mombasa, is famous for early Iron Age pottery, dating from about 200 A.D. It was made by Bantu farmers who migrated to the coast from inland.

The Kingdom of Wanga

The Luhya people of Western Province near the town of Kakamega are a loose-knit group of people descended from Bantu and Nilotic migrants into the area. There are probably around 18 different groups that speak the Luhya language. They were united in the 1600s by Wanga, who founded the kingdom named after him. Many Luhya came from the rich Ugandan kingdoms to the west of Lake Victoria, and legend says this is where Wanga came from. The Wanga kingdom flourished until the final years of the 19th century, when it became part of British East Africa.

THE COAST

The Kenyan coast and its islands have a different, and for many centuries, somewhat separate history from the interior. The two regions have been linked by trade, though, probably for as long as they have been populated. The Africans who settled on the coast also had links with the world beyond Africa, links that altered considerably the culture and history of the region. The Swahili people who live along the coast of Kenya today emerged as a distinct group due to the intermingling of Arabian, Persian, Indian, Portuguese, and African peoples. Islam, introduced by the Arabs not long after its foundation in 622 A.D., has particularly influenced Swahili culture.

The Swahili lived in stone-walled towns ruled over by men called sheikhs or sultans and worshiped at mosques. Wealthier citizens lived in houses more than one story high, ate off Chinese porcelain, wore silk cloth, and decorated their doors with gold and silver studs. The source of all this wealth was trade.

The island of Lamu has been inhabited for the last 2,000 years. Its position on the east coast made it a meeting place for generations of foreign traders.

Swahili was not used as a name for coastal East Africans until the 1800s. It was probably introduced by Omani Arabs.

ANCIENT TRADE ROUTES

Kenya's Indian Ocean coast was part of a flourishing African trade route that stretched from Mogadishu on the Somali coast in the north, to Sofala, Mozambique, in the south. Coastal settlements were outlets for goods from inland as well as for goods produced locally. An important link between Africa and Arabia, the Persian

Ode to Riches

The Swahili people have a long tradition of writing and reciting verse. Men and women created poems that were lyrical descriptions of their daily lives or events they had seen, or that advised others on how to behave. Originally based on the Arabic tradition of religious poetry, Swahili poets elaborated the form and incorporated elements of African ritual songs. Written examples of Swahili poetry date back 300 years but an oral tradition has existed for much longer. This 18th-century Swahili poem vividly describes just how well some Swahili merchants lived:

How many wealthy men have we not
*   seen*
Their lighted mansions glowed with
*   lamps of brass*
And crystal, til night seemed like the
*   very day*
Their homes were set with Chinese
*   porcelain*
And every cup and goblet was
*   engraved*
While, placed amid the glittering
*   ornaments,*

Great crystal pitchers gleamed
*   all luminous.*
The rails from which they hung the
*   rich brocade*
Were made—I swear by God, Source
*   of all wealth—*
Of teak and ebony, row upon row
*   of them,*
Rank upon rank with fabrics hung
*   and displayed.*
The men's halls hummed with chatter,
*   while within*
The women's quarters laughter
*   echoed loud.*
The noise of talk and merriment
*   of slaves*
Rang out, and cheerful shouts of
*   workmen rose...*

This is part of a longer poem, called *Utendi wa Inkishafi* (*The Soul's Awakening*). One of the greatest religious poems, it was written by Sayyid Abdallah bin Nasir (c. 1720–1810) to illustrate the vanity of earthly life. The poem is an account of the fall of the city-state of Pate.

Gulf, and India, the coast was visited by Greek merchants at least 2,000 years ago. *The Periplus of the Erythraean Sea* is a guidebook for traders written around 100 A.D. by a Greek merchant from Alexandria in northern Egypt. The Erythraean Sea was the Greek name for the Indian Ocean. The book mentions, though only vaguely, people and places on the Kenyan, Somalian, and Tanzanian coasts that were trading with ports along the Red Sea. The earliest Greek, Arab, and Egyptian visitors did not settle, however, and the first people to do so came much later—from the eighth and ninth centuries on.

Manda and Pate Island

The group of islands that included Pate and Lamu with their natural harbors, was one of the first developed regions in Kenya. Among the most prosperous early trading towns on the whole east African coast was Manda, an island port next to the island of Lamu. Exports included mangrove timber (for treeless Arabia), gold, ivory, leopard skins, and iron. Metalwork, textiles, fine pottery from as far away as China, and other luxury items were the main imports. African ivory was valued highly in China and India. *The Pate Chronicles* from Pate Island near Lamu relate how the town of Pate was founded in the eighth century by Arabs. In reality, there was probably already a settlement on the island. The ruins of a town, Shanga, which are at least 1,000 years old have been uncovered on the southside of the island. The town had a seawall, palace, and cemetery with more than 300 tombs. Shanga was abandoned in the 14th century, perhaps after an attack by invaders.

This vase, found at Fort Jesus, Mombasa, was brought to Kenya from China and dates to the Sung dynasty (A.D. 960–1279). The Chinese inscription indicates the type of tea that it held.

MEDIEVAL TRADE IN EAST AFRICA

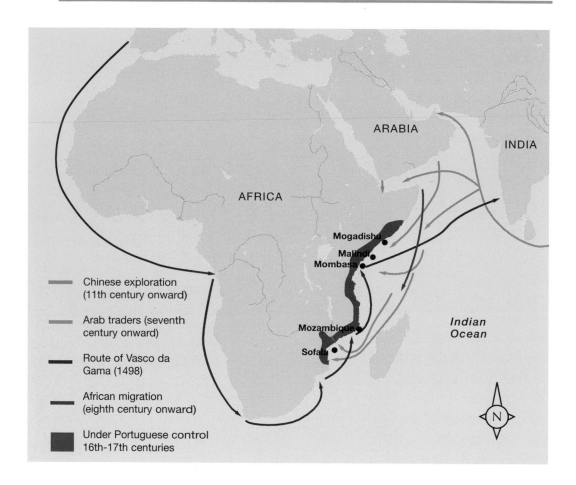

Key (legend):

Chinese exploration
(11th century onward)

Arab traders (seventh
century onward)

Route of Vasco da
Gama (1498)

African migration
(eighth century onward)

Under Portuguese control
16th-17th centuries

Map labels: ARABIA, INDIA, AFRICA, Mogadishu, Malindi, Mombasa, Mozambique, Sofala, Indian Ocean, N

Arab and Chinese traders from the north and east respectively preceded European explorers, the first of whom reached East Africa in the late 15th century.

No one knows for sure. Pate was famous for the multi-colored silk cloth its residents produced, and it, too, became wealthy through trade with Arabs, Indians, and later the Portuguese. At times it controlled much of the immediate coastlands and islands, including Lamu, which was often allied to Pate.

The Chinese, who by the mid-15th century had the world's most advanced fleet, visited the coasts of Somalia and Kenya. A giraffe was brought back from Africa by the Chinese admiral Cheng Ho in 1414 and a further expedition was sent in the 1430s, which traded finely made Chinese goods for African spices.

THE ARRIVAL OF THE PORTUGUESE

Farther south, another settlement was increasing its control over the trade routes, eventually overtaking the northern ports in size and importance. In existence since at least 1000 A.D., Mombasa also grew rich through trade, rivaled for a while by Malindi on the coast. The port grew steadily in importance until in 1588, despite strong resistance, it was conquered by the Portuguese. The Europeans were eager to dominate the profitable trade routes all along the east coast from Sofala, now in Mozambique, to Mogadishu, in modern Somalia. The Portuguese came to be known as *Afriti* (devils) for their plundering and destroying of towns, but their control of the coast was never complete or permanent. By imposing heavy duties, they made trading unprofitable for any ex-

A wall drawing of ships made by Portuguese sailors at Fort Jesus, Mombasa, in the 17th century.

cept themselves, and Kenya's ports in particular began to weaken. After nearly losing Mombasa to coastal Africans allied with the Sultan of Malindi, the Portuguese made the port the headquarters of their activities in east Africa.

They built the stronghold that still stands there today, Fort Jesus (*see* p. 40).

Revolt in Mombasa

In 1593 the Portuguese installed their ally Sheikh Ahmad as the ruler of Mombasa. As the Swahili ruler of Malindi on the coast, he had long been a rival of Mombasa's. Sheikh Ahmad became dissatisfied with the Portuguese though, so local officials conspired with coastal Africans to have him killed. He was replaced by

Slavery and the Slave Trade

East Africa, including Kenya, suffered from the evils of the slave trade—as did west Africa—which peaked in the 19th century. Slavery and the slave trade were not new to the region: People had been enslaved before, sold, captured, or traded to Arabs or sent to Arab states to work. By the 1800s, however, demand for slaves had greatly increased, and more people were enslaved than ever before. European nations and settlers in the Americas had been busy expanding into new territories, farming lands with favorable climates. They started "mass producing" profitable cash crops such as sugar on large plantations. Essential to the whole business was a supply of cheap slave labor. Slaves from East Africa ended up in French sugar plantations on the Indian Ocean islands of Réunion and Mauritius, Portuguese plantations in Brazil, or Arab clove and coconut groves on the East African coast. By 1840 more than 40,000 people from the coast were being sold at the chief slave market at Zanzibar every year; by 1860 the figure was more than 60,000 a year. The majority came from lands south of present-day Kenya's coast, but several thousand at least must have been enslaved in Kenya. People were taken largely from along the coast and from western Kenya to slave markets in Uganda then to Zanzibar. The Kamba were the main Kenyan people involved in the slave trade. They lived, and still do, in the dry grasslands inland of the coast north of the Athi River. Unable to rely on an uncertain rainfall to provide for their crops or animals, they had begun trading with their neighbors at an early date. The most important trade was in ivory, which they obtained by smelting iron arrowheads and

Slavery in East Africa

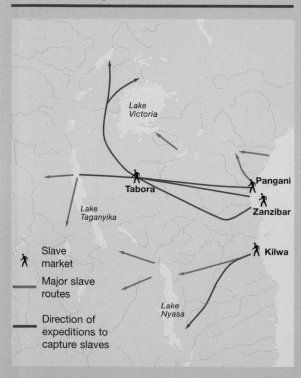

Lake Victoria

Lake Taganyika

Tabora

Pangani

Zanzibar

Kilwa

Lake Nyasa

Slave market

Major slave routes

Direction of expeditions to capture slaves

perfecting the killing of elephants with poison arrows. They also traded in slaves, though, until Arab and Swahili people started making their own raids to make still more money. Equipped with guns, they preyed mercilessly upon those without firearms. One witness to a slave-raiding trip described it with horror:

"We passed a woman tied by the neck to a tree and dead...we saw others tied up in a similar manner, and one lying in the path shot or stabbed for she was in a pool of blood. The explanation we got invariably was that the Arab who owned these victims was enraged at losing his money by the slaves becoming unable to march."

Those were the words of the famous Scottish explorer David Livingstone. He did not witness this in Kenya, but it is likely to be an accurate description of similar events there. As the 19th century ended, slavery ceased as well. Although many people in Europe and America had campaigned against slavery and the slave trade, an important cause of its decline was the end of its profitability. Instead of enslaving African citizens, Europeans had turned instead to colonizing the continent of Africa in the search for new markets and cheap raw materials for the goods that they were producing in the factories of Europe.

Lords of the Savannas

From the 1600s to the 1900s the Maasai people dominated much of the grasslands of what are now Kenya and Tanzania, through. Many important caravan routes passed through this area, traveling between central Africa and the coast. Traders who crossed their lands had to pay for safe passage, and the Maasai were feared in battle. The men were trained from an early age to always show great courage, whether facing a lion or a human enemy. The Maasai were not a single united people, though; leadership was in the hands of groups of elders. Some groups had religious leaders called *laibons*, and in the mid-1800s one such man, Mbatian (c. 1820–1889), nearly succeeded in uniting the Maasai into a single nation. Quarrels after Mbatian's death over who should succeed him weakened Maasai resistance to the British, who were able to move into power.

During the 18th century the seafaring Omanis from eastern Arabia formed a substantial empire in Oman and East Africa (the two regions were separated after 1861). For a period the Omani capital was at Zanzibar. The Omani sultan then declared Zanzibar independent from Oman, founding the Sultanate of Zanzibar.

his son, who was educated, raised, and converted to Christianity by the Portuguese in Goa, on the west coast of India. However, the son quarreled with the Portuguese, though, returning to his Muslim roots and leading a revolt against them in 1631. The revolt failed, and the sheikh's son lived out his days as a pirate.

Omani Rule

In 1698 Mombasa was finally taken from the Portuguese by Omani Arab and Pate troops. This was after a 33-month siege saw the death of nearly all the Portuguese in the town plus several hundred loyal Swahilis. Mombasa became the center of the Omani efforts to take control of the region. The Omanis held the port until the mid-18th century, except for a brief period (1728–1729) when Portugal regained control. Within a few decades, the Mazrui rulers of Mombasa declared themselves independent of Oman. The Mazrui family grew powerful, extending their control over other coastal regions, including the island of Pemba to the south. The Omanis retook Mombasa in the first half of the 19th century but lost it to the British in 1895.

BRITISH COLONIALISM

In the 1800s Africa was carved up into colonies by European nations as they attempted to secure markets for their goods, such as cloth, that were being produced in newly-established factories. They also wanted to secure the supply of cheap raw materials for the same factories. Fearful that others would get there first, by the 1880s European contact with Africa had become a scramble to control territory. European nations played out long-standing political rivalries in Africa. New African borders were decided by officials in faraway cities who had never even visited the lands they marked out. The borders between Kenya and Tanzania, and a part of the border between Somalia and Kenya still look as though they were drafted with a pencil and ruler. A bend in the southern border puts Mount Kilimanjaro in Tanzania (formerly German East Africa) instead of Kenya. It was rumored at the time that the

By the late 1840s one Kamba man, Kivoli, was known as the "merchant prince." He was the most powerful of the Kamba long-distance traders. Long caravans of ivory, led by his agents, made their way from east-central Kenya to Mombasa.

Officials of the Imperial British East Africa Company (IBEAC) make a treaty with the Kikuyu people. Such treaties, which often misled Africans, ended attacks on European settlements, enabled the British to build the railroad across East Africa, thus ensuring their trade interests in the region.

mountain had very nearly been British territory until the Kaiser, the German ruler and the British queen's grandson, had expressed a liking for the mountain.

To secure access to Uganda, Britain claimed Kenya as the British East Africa protectorate (colony) in 1895, although they signed no legal treaties with any of the people living there nor bought any of the land. Facing a fleet of Omani warships, the sultan of Mombasa had once asked a passing British warship to protect the port. The captain agreed, but his decision was overturned by his superiors, and Mombasa was abandoned to the Omanis two years later, in 1826. The British leased a 10-mile (16-km) wide strip of coastal land running as far north as Lamu from the Sultan of Zanzibar in 1895. His control over the land had been established in 1885 by a treaty with the Germans. Mumia, the king of Wanga, had no idea his realm was to be included in the colony until an official arrived to set up headquarters there in 1894. One treaty was made with the Maasai *laibons* in 1904. It restricted them to two reserves linked by a strip of land along which they could migrate with their herds. The agreement was not honored by the Europeans, however, and the strip of land was the first to be lost to settlers. When the northern parts of the reserve were lost, the Maasai were left with only dry grasslands in the south.

More than 200,000 Kenyan porters and soldiers were sent to Tanzania (German East Africa) during World War I. Below are guards from the King's African Rifles at Njombe in Tanzania.

Resistance

The colonists were strongly resisted by the Africans, particularly the Nandi of western Kenya. The Mazrui rebelled in Mombasa in 1895–1896, delaying the construction of the Uganda railroad. British, and sometimes Luhya, troops were sent to put down Kipsigis, Embu, Gusii, and others. Some British people thought their country was engaged in the task of "civilizing" Africa, though they had little knowledge of the continent. Although a few politicians also professed these beliefs, their aims were shown to be false by the way the colonies were run: as businesses that profited Europeans, not Africans. The Imperial British East Africa Imperial (IBEAC), a commercial company, was given the control of British East Africa, which it occupied on behalf of the British government. The construction of the railroad from Mombasa to Kisumu (*see* p. 66) and Lake Victoria was in their hands, though millions of pounds were supplied by the British government. By 1916 Europeans controlled 5,790 square miles (15,000 sq. km) of prime land.

Mumia (c. 1850–1949), king of Wanga during the colonial period, supported the British and became very powerful. He was made "paramount chief" of a huge district in western Kenya. Unpopular with non-Luo people, however, he was forced to retire in 1926. In his final years, he became a supporter of independence.

Prophecies of Doom

By the early 1800s the Nandi of the western highlands had developed a complex system of government. Previously, each of the several smaller Nandi groups had their own ruling council of elders, chosen for their wisdom and military skill. A Maasai man called Barsabotwo came to live among the Nandi, and his advice helped them win many battles. He became the first central authority of the Nandi, whom the elders would consult on all important matters. In the 1880s, their legendary leader, Kimnyolei arap Samoei, Barsabotwo's grandson and successor, warned his people of a fire-breathing snake that would run along the escarpment to drink in the great lake and of the white people who would conquer the Nandi. His prophecies came true with the arrival of the Lunatic Line and the white settlers who followed. Nevertheless, the Nandi bravely defended their homelands from 1894 until they were finally defeated in 1906. Samoei had agreed to meet the British to discuss peace. They betrayed his trust and killed him, then defeated the leaderless Nandi.

Many Africans were moved to cramped reserves with poor land. Others suddenly found themselves squatters and were forced to pay rent with their labor on white farms. Those who were reluctant to go or who resisted were massacred. Towns sprung up around official administrative centers and mission stations. The towns of Machakos, Murang'a, and Mumias all began as IBEAC company posts. The capital of the colony was switched from Mombasa to Nairobi in 1907 to be nearer the "White Highlands," as the settled lands came to be called. In 1920 British East Africa was renamed Kenya. When gold was discovered at Kakamega north of Kisumu in 1931, more Kenyans were ousted from their land.

The Railroad

The railroad was the turning point in Kenyan, and east African, history. It brought settlers to African farmlands, and was vital to the colonization of the region. Politicians encouraged settlers to make the fertile highlands and lusher grasslands their homes. Tracts of the best land, advertised abroad and sold on easy terms, were set aside for whites only. Many people from Gujarat province in India traveled to east Africa to work on the railroad. After it was finished they set up businesses along the railroad route: Many of their descendants still remain.

Workers digging the cross-Kenyan railroad

The Poll Tax

In 1906, a law was made that tax had to be paid on every African's home. A later law added a poll tax that every adult had to pay as well as the "hut tax." Suddenly, besides supporting their families, an increasingly difficult task, Kenyans had to find a way to earn cash. They were not allowed to grow the profitable cash crops that the settlers farmed, such as coffee and tea, and so were forced to look for work at the white-owned factories and farms. Africans found themselves working for low wages and under bad conditions. The settlers did not pay any direct tax, even though they could well afford to. They were even bailed out by the British government when their markets were hit badly by the Great Depression, which followed the Wall Street Crash of 1929.

As a colony, Kenya was ruled by a governor and a legislative council, which was largely controlled by officials representing the settlers' interests. After much campaigning, Asian Kenyans were allowed to elect their own official to the council. Africans, however, were not allowed to have their own council members until the 1940s. Even then, African officials were not elected but appointed by the governor.

The First Revolts

All these injustices led, inevitably, to revolts against white colonialists. In the 1920s the moderate Kikuyu Association was formed. Harry Thuku (see p. 38) founded the more radical Young Kikuyu Association, later the Kikuyu Central Association (KCA). The main demands were for better work conditions and the return of Kikuyu land. Jomo Kenyatta, the KCA's general secretary, was one of the most outspoken critics of colonialism. In 1944 the Kenya African Union (KAU) was founded. Thuku and Kenyatta were among the first leaders. They wanted to create a nationwide independence movement, but support was still dominated by the Kikuyu. This domination was to continue when Kenyatta became president (see p. 71).

Kenyans worked as front-line porters and soldiers during World War I (1914–1918). Of these, a quarter were killed. During World War II (1939–1945) they fought the Japanese in Burma (Myanmar) and helped drive the Italians out of Ethiopia.

Growing Anger

In a pamphlet published in Britain in 1945, Jomo Kenyatta warned: "What we do demand is a fundamental change in the present political, economic, and social relationship between Europeans and Africans...the Africans make their claim for justice now, in order that a bloodier and more destructive justice may not be inevitable in time to come."

The British government said they were preparing Kenya for independence, but claimed that the Kenyans were not yet ready to govern themselves. In the late 1940s, some members of the KAU, frustrated with the pace of change, turned to direct action. Many joined the Kenya Land Freedom Army, or Freedom Fighters, who came to be better known as Mau Mau. Members were mostly Kikuyu, but also Meru, Embu, Kamba, and Maasai. They organized surprise attacks against settlers' farms and police stations. They also attacked fellow Kenyans who did not want to change anything or who supported the British.

Police transport suspected members of the Mau Mau to a "screening" compound during a surprise street check in Nairobi during the 1950s.

In 1951 Mau Mau was declared unlawful and two years later was banned, but this had little impact on the rebels' activities. They went into hiding in the forests of the Aberdares and Mount Kenya. In 1952 a state of emergency was declared, troops were flown in from Britain, and a huge crackdown began. Hundreds of Kikuyus were imprisoned, often after mass arrests, then detained without trial. Kenyatta and other leaders of the KAU were thrown into jail, though they denied organizing the rebel-

Kenyan protesters demand independence during the 1950s.

lion. Camps were set up to control the movements of civilians who were forced to live there. Misleadingly called "protected villages," the camps were often behind barbed wire. After four years of fierce resistance in central Kenya, the Mau Mau uprising was put down. Its leaders, such as Dedan Kimathi and General China, had been killed or captured, and more than 10,000 Freedom Fighters as well as at least 2,000 Kikuyu civilians had died. Around 100,000 people had been herded into camps by the British. Fifty-eight whites and Asians had died during the uprising, in addition to around 50 British soldiers.

The uprising forced officials to accept the need to talk with Africans about independence. Pressure from countries such as the Soviet Union and the United States also helped. In 1957 African Kenyans were allowed to vote in their first elections, but only if they could read, earned above a certain amount of money, or owned a certain amount of land. The elected Africans refused to accept their posts until all adults were allowed to vote. Finally, after many more meetings and conferences, universal elections were planned for 1963. The party that won would run Kenya as an independent country.

In 1960 the Kenya African National Union (KANU) was formed, dominated by the Luo and Kikuyu tribes. Soon afterward the more moderate Kenya African Democratic Union (KADU), formed, aiming to represent people of other groups.

Kenyan Indians arrive at Luton Airport north of London in February 1968. The British government's proposed withdrawal of British citizenship from Asian Kenyans led many to move to Britain, fearing intimidation in Kenya itself.

UHURU

Kenya finally achieved Uhuru (freedom) in 1963. The elections were won by the Kenya African National Union (KANU), formed a few years earlier in 1960 and led by Jomo Kenyatta (*see* box opposite). Within a year, Kenya had abandoned the British model of democracy and become a republic with Kenyatta at the helm as president. The new leaders inherited complex problems that needed attention, one of the most troublesome of which was uniting their citizens into a single Kenyan nation.

With the upheavals and strife of the 68 years of foreign rule still fresh, Kenyan politicians felt it more important to foster national unity than to encourage independent political groups. Kenyans needed to pull together (*harambee*) for the country to survive. The main opposition party (KADU) broke up and joined KANU's ranks in 1964. The only other opposition party was banned after a disturbance at a public meeting attended by Kenyatta in Kisumu. At least ten people were killed after the police opened fire.

Harambee

After Kenya became a republic in 1964 an effort was made for political and social unity—or what was known as *harambee*. Local meetings and fundraising events encouraged important locals to make donations toward health care and educational programs. Many *harambee* schools were built and equipped, producing a national feeling of local self-help. While some people became *harambee* supporters just to gain prestige, the movement remains a force for good.

Burning Spear

Fittingly, Jomo Kenyatta, Kenya's first independent leader, was born at around the same time that Kenya came into being as the British East Africa protectorate in the late 1890s. His name was Kamau Ngengi, but he changed it to Jomo, meaning Burning Spear in Kikuyu, and Kenyatta, after the beaded belt that he wore around his waist. As a boy, he was educated at a mission school; as an adult, he traveled to England in 1931 to study at the London School of Economics. While there, he wrote *Facing Mount Kenya*. His book reveals the structure and values of Kikuyu society, and the impact of colonialism, and asserts the ability of Africans to govern themselves. He was an important figure among Kenyans forced to live in exile. When Kenyatta returned home in 1946, he was given a hero's welcome. His imprisonment from 1952 to 1961 cemented his status in the eyes of the people, and he was made president of KANU before he was even released. After he became president of independent Kenya, Kenyatta surprised many people with his attempts to make peace with the settler community. His wisdom and courage earned him the title of *Mzee* (Elder), but he became

increasingly remote from his people in later years and controlled the country with an iron hand. Kenyatta's legacy is mixed, since he introduced laws that made it legal to detain people without trial and turned Kenya into a one-party state in all but name. Moreover, the domination of Kenyatta's Kikuyu people was resented by other groups, and decidedly reversed by Kenyatta's successor. He was always held in high esteem, though, and at his funeral, mourners filed past his coffin for days.

After this, at election time the only candidates people could vote for were KANU ones. Kenyatta was voted in as president three times before he died in 1978.

FROM ONE-PARTY TO MULTIPARTY POLITICS

On Kenyatta's death, vice-president Daniel arap Moi become president. He formally declared Kenya a one-party state in 1982—although this had effectively been the case since the late 1960s. In the same year, a military coup led by largely Luo members of the air force tried to overthrow him. In Nairobi, chaos ruled for a few days. The radio station was taken over; shops, in particular Asian shops, were looted; and people were killed. The aftermath of the unsuccessful rebellion saw around 3,000 people arrested and the air force disbanded. Nairobi University was closed down because many of the students had supported the coup. When peace returned, the university reopened and many prisoners were released, but the events set a pattern of rebellion followed by repression that was to become common. In the years to follow, members of the Kenyan parliament who disagreed with Moi were detained; several critics of the government also died mysteriously.

Daniel arap Moi, Kenya's former vice-president is sworn in as president on the death of Kenyatta in 1978.

World opinion started to turn against Moi's government. In 1987, 1995, and 1997, the international human rights organization Amnesty International published reports condemning the government for the imprisonment of people without trial and for torture. Moi

Today these giant aluminum tusks , which span Moi Avenue in Mombasa, are seen as a symbol of Kenya. But they were originally erected in 1953 to celebrate the coronation of Queen Elizabeth II of Britain.

In 1998 the U.S. embassy in Nairobi was destroyed by a car bomb. Two hundred and twelve people were killed and thousands more injured. The United States government accused 17 men of planning the attack, led by Saudi exile Osama bin Laden.

responded to such pressure by releasing all political prisoners in 1989, and he promised not to arrest those political exiles who returned home.

The following year antigovernment riots swept Nairobi, Kisumu, and the Central Highlands. In 1992 continued pressure at home and from abroad finally forced Moi to allow opposition parties to form. Moi won his fourth five-year term as president at the election held later that year, despite facing opponents for the first time. Opposition parties have had limited success, however, since they divide the anti-KANU voters into competing camps. No one party has emerged that is popular enough to defeat KANU, which is better organized and better financed than all its other rivals.

In 1997, on the anniversary of the pro-democracy riots of 1990, rallies were held across Kenya to demand

In July 1989, facing international criticism of elephant poaching in Kenya, President Moi appointed the esteemed paleontologist Richard Leakey as head of the Kenyan Wildlife Service. Leakey's transformation of the KWS drew in huge investment from overseas and saved Kenyan elephants and rhinos from extinction.

reforms limiting the powers of government. Security forces responded harshly, attacking passersby, and millions of TV viewers watched as officers even attacked women carrying children. Before the end of the year, however, laws had been introduced that made the detention of prisoners without trial illegal, and the police have been ordered to stop disrupting peaceful rallies. In January 1998, Moi began his fifth and final term as president.

KENYA TODAY

The Republic of Kenya has one house of representatives, the National Assembly (Bunge). Two hundred and ten members of the assembly are elected by the people; 12 are selected by the president, his party, and the opposition parties. The president and ministers together make up the main ruling body: the cabinet. The cabinet is appointed by the president. Each minister leads a ministry concerned with a particular area of activity. There are ministries (government departments) of water and energy, the environment, and science and technology, for example. The number of ministries has been recently cut down from more than 20 to fewer than 15.

Elections for both president and the National Assembly are held every five years. All Kenyans over the age of 18 can vote directly for the person they want to

Despite the size of Kenya's population, its system of government is relatively simple, with power concentrated in the hands of the president and his cabinet.

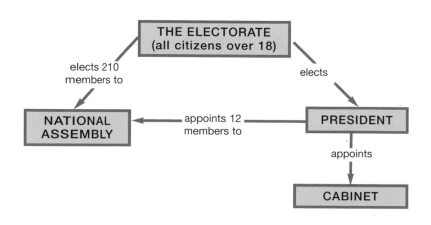

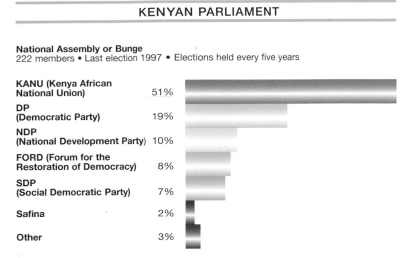

KENYAN PARLIAMENT

National Assembly or Bunge
222 members • Last election 1997 • Elections held every five years

Party	%
KANU (Kenya African National Union)	51%
DP (Democratic Party)	19%
NDP (National Development Party)	10%
FORD (Forum for the Restoration of Democracy)	8%
SDP (Social Democratic Party)	7%
Safina	2%
Other	3%

Despite Kenya becoming a multiparty democracy in 1991, Moi's KANU party won an overall majority in 1997.

be president. To win, in addition to getting the most votes, a candidate must get 25 percent of the total votes in at least five of Kenya's eight provinces.

After independence the Kikuyu dominated Kenyan politics and business. They suffered the most damage during the colonial era, and many of the early nationalists were Kikuyu. But after independence attempts to make up for these wrongs led to the concentration of power in their hands, and other people in Kenya increasingly resisted this. With Moi's arrival, the focus of political power shifted to his ethnic group, the Kalenjin, and other minority groups, although today the Kalenjin make up no more than about 12 percent of the population (*see* p. 10)

Constitutional Amendments

Since the first constitution was adopted in 1963, the National Assembly has amended it on different occasions: to make Kenya a republic (1964), a one-party state (1982), and now a multiparty state (1991). More changes in 1997 granted all political parties equal access to the media, and made detention without trial illegal. Also, opposition parties were given the right to participate in selecting the 12 nominated members of the National Assembly.

In 1986 Moi introduced the voting-line system. At an election, people had to stand in a public line to vote for a candidate. This made it much easier to control people's votes and to pressure them to vote for the "right" candidate. The voting line was abolished in 1990.

The Economy

"Only a medicine man gets rich by sleeping."

Kambu proverb

Kenya has the most important economy in east Africa, yet many Kenyans live in poverty. Economically the country has undergone huge changes in the last 100 years. The colonial era left the country dependent on cash crops sold to Western markets, usually as raw materials. Crops such as coffee and tea are prone to sudden price swings, while others, such as cotton and sisal, do not make as much profit as products manufactured from them. The economy still relies on cash crops, although today tourism is even more important. Cash crops bring in much-needed foreign exchange but can also be affected by factors beyond the control of Kenyan business, government, and farmers, such as bad weather or price changes. Since independence much has been done to improve the situation. The government has encouraged Kenyans to set up their own businesses, and new, high-earning crops, like cut flowers, have been tried out successfully.

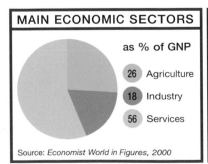

MAIN ECONOMIC SECTORS

as % of GNP

26 Agriculture

18 Industry

56 Services

Source: *Economist World in Figures, 2000*

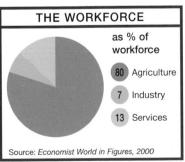

THE WORKFORCE

as % of workforce

80 Agriculture

7 Industry

13 Services

Source: *Economist World in Figures, 2000*

Kenya's economy is still overwhelmingly geared toward production of basic agricultural products, such as sugarcane, shown here being harvested.

MAJOR ECONOMIC SECTORS

The vast majority of Kenyans are involved in agriculture as farmers, animal herders, or both. Many grow crops or raise animals that are sold at markets both within Kenya and abroad. Large plantations and ranches also export produce. Cash crops were once produced by a few large plantations, but within the last 20 years many small farmers have been brought into the farming economy, often working together in cooperatives. The manufacturing and service sectors are much larger than those of countries with similar low income levels. Kenya's manufacturing sector is also the most diversified in the region. Wealthy settlers in the early 20th century needed something to spend their money on, and this triggered the growth of manufacturing industries in Kenya. Today, demand for manufactured goods is kept high by wealthy Africans as well as by the few non-African settlers who remain or who have moved to the country since independence. Service industries are those that provide services, such as hotel accommodation or a meal in a restaurant. In Kenya, this sector of the economy is dominated by tourism. Tourism is so important to the economy that it has been called Kenya's biggest export.

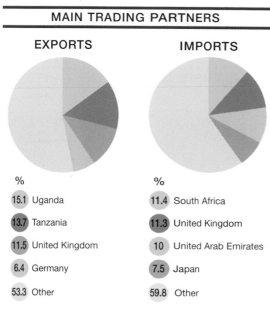

MAIN TRADING PARTNERS

EXPORTS

IMPORTS

%
15.1 Uganda
13.7 Tanzania
11.5 United Kingdom
6.4 Germany
53.3 Other

%
11.4 South Africa
11.3 United Kingdom
10 United Arab Emirates
7.5 Japan
59.8 Other

Source: *Economist World in Figures, 2000*

AGRICULTURE

More than three-quarters of Kenyans make their living from the land. At least half of these are subsistence producers. A subsistence producer is someone who grows or rears enough food for his or her family to eat. Surpluses might be sold for cash, or bartered, exchanged for other goods. The Okiek, for example, exchange the honey they collect from wild bees for meat and dairy products provided by their neighbors, the Maasai. On the coast and around Lake Victoria fishing is an important activity, providing food for much of the surrounding regions.

On the Hoof

There are many more farmers than pastoralists (animal herders) in Kenya, but the pastoralists make use of much more land than crop farmers. Less dependent on high rainfall, they are able to keep animals all over vast tracts of the savannas as well as in the drier scrublands, often moving with their herds in search of water and pasture. Some even manage to eke out a living in the semideserts of the far north of the country.

There are more than 14 million cattle in Kenya. Some are slaughtered, their meat sold or eaten, and their skin made into leather. Most are kept for their milk, which is drunk or used to make butter and cheese. To many pastoralists who rely solely on their herd for food, their animals are an important investment that, if killed, will

EXPORTS

IMPORTS

EXPORTS ($m)	
Tea	411
Coffee	287
Horticultural products	234
Petroleum	122
Others	905
Total (including others)	1,959

IMPORTS ($m)	
Petroleum and products	493
Industrial machinery	477
Motor vehicles and chassis	244
Iron and steel	183
Others	1,881
Total (including others)	3,278

Source: *Economist World in Figures, 2000*

Kenya's exports are dominated by cash crops, while its major imports are mainly manufactured goods and oil. Below, a Maasai pastoralist from north central Kenya.

Land Reform

After Kenya became independent, the British government and the World Bank bought many of the settlers' farms in the Western Highlands. Up to 500,000 Africans were settled on these lands, which they purchased with loans repayable over a 30-year period. These highly fertile lands can often be farmed intensively, such as on the banana plantation above, where the soil beneath the banana plants is being prepared for a different crop. Most land in Kenya is now owned by Kenyans, but many remain landless. Around a million acres of the best farmland was bought by African farmers to make large holdings. So some Kikuyu found themselves no longer squatters on European-owned farms but squatters on African-owned farms instead.

Pastoralist land use presents special problems. Land may appear to be empty and unused but still be an important part of a pastoralist's range. Dry grasslands can only support small numbers of widely scattered people. Today the Kenyan government holds the land in trust for the benefit of the residents, and it is administered by local council officials.

only yield a one-time lump sum. If kept alive, however, the animals still provide food and can also reproduce, enlarging the herd.

Large ranches with hundreds of cattle exist in Kenya, either owned by a few wealthy people or the government, or run as cooperatives by groups of herders. Many farmers, particularly in western Kenya, also keep cattle, for the most part just one or two animals for their milk and meat. Pigs, sheep, and goats are kept as well as cattle, but they are far less common. In the Rift Valley, farmers often keep a few sheep for their meat and wool.

HOW KENYA USES ITS LAND

Desert

Forest

Pasture

Croplands

Farming

Only 15 percent of Kenya has sufficiently reliable rainfall for farming—about 21.5 million acres (8.7 million hectares) of the country. Another 875,000 acres (354,200 hectares), or 0.2 percent of the land, could be farmed if it were supplied with water, or irrigated. However, irrigating land is expensive and few Kenyans can afford it, so only around 0.1 percent of Kenya is irrigated. The government encourages farmers to irrigate by offering loans, and plans have been made to build more government-run projects. Already, the huge Bura project on the Tana River provides water for cotton growers.

Cropland is largely limited to the tropical east coast, the area around Lake Victoria, and parts of the Central Highlands.

LAND USE

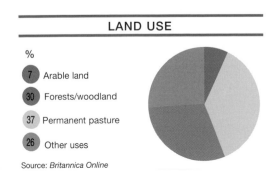

%
7 Arable land
30 Forests/woodland
37 Permanent pasture
26 Other uses

Source: *Britannica Online*

Settlers introduced coffee, tea, wheat, and cattle ranching to Kenya. For many years, only settlers were allowed to farm profitable cash crops like coffee and tea. Of the cash crops, Asians were only allowed to farm sugarcane; many became important sugar producers.

For food, people still grow the hardy cereal crops sorghum and millet, especially in areas where rainfall is poor. The most important food crop in Kenya is corn (maize), closely followed by bananas in the Central Highlands and western Kenya. Corn and bananas are not native to Kenya. They were introduced to the coast and to east-central Africa hundreds of years ago by European visitors. Wheat is another important food crop, but more is imported, or bought from farmers in other countries, than is grown in Kenya.

Cash Crops

Although most Kenyan farmers are subsistence producers, more than 1.7 million grow cash crops for sale at markets. These farmers have small plots of land, mostly less than several acres in size. For this reason they are called smallholders. Nearly 4,000 others own large farms, ranches, or plantations.

The main crops grown by both small and large cash croppers are tea and coffee. Coffee was the most important cash crop in the past but tea overtook it in the 1990s. Because coffee prices can rise one year and then plummet the next, many farmers have turned to more stable or profitable crops. Some foreign companies still own large tea plantations in Central and Western Kenya—the British company Brooke Bond, for instance. Most tea is grown on smallholdings or cooperative farms (see box this page). Other important crops are chrysanthemums

The Tea Plantations

Kenya's tea plantations, which account for 20 to 30 percent of the country's export earnings, are largely located in the Western Highlands, around the towns of Kisii and Kericho. Here the climate, with its moderate temperatures, bright sunshine, and light daily rain, is ideal for tea-growing. Leaves are picked every 17 days and each worker farms one area of land, and is responsible for picking up to 220 lb (100 kg) of tea a day. Recently large multinational companies have pulled out of Kenyan tea plantations, and they have been taken over by small landowners. These landowners now produce 66 percent of Kenya's tea, selling it to the Kenyan Tea Development Authority, which then markets it abroad.

Horticulture

One of the most rapidly expanding sectors of the Kenyan economy is horticulture—the growing of fruit, vegetables, and flowers—largely for the export market. The highlands of Kenya are perfect for horticulture. After tea and coffee, horticultural crops are the most important Kenyan export. Every week more than 2,000 tons of cut flowers, fruit, and vegetables are exported to the Middle East and Europe. Kenya is now the fourth largest exporter of cut flowers in the world. In 1997 more than 38,500 tons of cut flowers were exported to Europe, which amounts to over 5 million stems a day. Nearly half of the fruit and vegetables goes to the United Kingdom, where the most popular Kenyan flowers are roses. Smallholders, often organised in co-operatives, grow most of the fruit and vegetables, including lettuce, tomatoes, cucumbers, garlic, leeks, and carrots. Pineapples are grown on large plantations owned by a U.S. firm.

(also called pyrethrums), not for cut flowers but for pyrethrum. This chemical is extracted from chrysanthemum flowers and used to make insecticides. The main customer for pyrethrum is the United States. Recently, however, more and more farmers in the United States and elsewhere have started using biological controls like pest-eating insects. As a result, the demand for pyrethrum has fallen. Other nations, particularly those with limited funds and those concerned about the environment, are increasing their demand for dried pyrethrum flowers. Pyrethrum is considered to be better for the environment than expensive artificial pesticides.

Along the coast of Lake Victoria and the Indian Ocean, fish are an important food and market item. More fish sold in Kenya's markets are from Lake Victoria than from the coast.

Sugar

Sugar is a major crop in western Kenya. It is both sold as cane and made into refined sugar, which is used as a food ingredient. Smallholders and cooperatives sell their crops to factories for processing. Most of the sugar is sold in Kenya. There is rarely an official surplus for export, so Kenya often imports sugar to meet demand. These imports are usually much cheaper than Kenyan-grown sugar, and this makes it difficult for Kenyan farmers to sell their produce. Every year unknown amounts of Kenyan sugar are illegally exported to neighboring countries. In 1998 the government increased the tax on imported sugar to help Kenyan farmers compete. Ministers promised to stop sugar imports completely if producers stopped exporting illegally to other countries.

One sugar refinery in western Kenya made "gasohol," an alternative fuel for cars, created from sugar molasses converted into alcohol and mixed with gasoline. Gasohol was sold at gas stations in Nairobi for a while. Problems with supply, failed sugar crops, and high costs halted production in the early 1990s. There are plans to use sugar to generate electricity instead.

While India is the world's largest producer of tea, in 1995 and 1996 Kenya exported more tea than any other country in the world. Production faced setbacks due to droughts in 1997, but Kenya may soon recover its position as the world's largest tea exporter.

Growing Together

In the 1940s African farmers in Kenya started to get together in groups to sell their produce. They could make better deals with buyers as a group. Today, more than 2.5 million Kenyans belong to around 5,000 cooperatives. These farmers produce more than 60 percent of all the crops grown in Kenya. Being a member of a cooperative gives a farmer access to education, training, and information that he or she would not otherwise be able to afford. Like harambee societies (see page 70), many cooperatives charge membership fees to build up funds. Members are allowed to borrow money from the cooperative and use it to invest in seeds, fertilizers, or irrigation, or to pay school fees or hospital bills. Members can also save with and borrow from the Cooperative Bank of Kenya. Kenyan women are active in setting up their own farming cooperatives, including pastoralist women who have never farmed before.

MAJOR INDUSTRIES

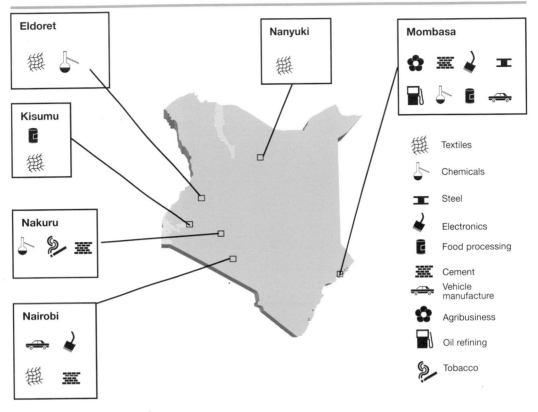

Eldoret

Nanyuki

Mombasa

Kisumu

Nakuru

Nairobi

Textiles
Chemicals
Steel
Electronics
Food processing
Cement
Vehicle manufacture
Agribusiness
Oil refining
Tobacco

INDUSTRY AND TRADE

With a good transportation structure and a reputation as a safe investment, Kenya has seen its industry flourish. Mombasa is still the busiest port on Africa's east coast, handling more than 7 million tons of goods a year. Goods from Kenya and its neighbors—Tanzania, Uganda, Burundi, Rwanda, and the Democratic Republic of the Congo (formerly Zaire)—leave Africa from Mombasa. Only a few hundred thousand people are employed in manufacturing, though, and half of Kenya's industries are owned by foreigners. The United Kingdom is the most important foreign investor, followed by the United States. Since independence, the government has made a huge effort to make the economy more self-reliant and less dependent on foreign investment and markets.

Kenyan industry is concentrated in the capital Nairobi and the country's main port, Mombasa.

In the 1990s drought severely affected the amount of corn farmers could grow, and grain had to be imported to prevent famine.

Manufacturing

Kenya's main manufacturing industries are based on processing, or making products from, crops. Pineapples are canned and juiced, and sugar is refined. Crude oil is imported, mainly from the United Arab Emirates, and made into petroleum at oil refineries. A large oil refinery at Mombasa pipes petroleum directly to Nairobi. There are plans to extend the pipeline to Lake Victoria. Kenya also produces paper, books, chemicals, glass, ceramics, rubber, leather goods, and textiles. Cars, trucks, and minibuses are put together in factories from imported parts. The vehicles are sold in Kenya and other African countries. The once-flourishing textile industry slumped in the late 1990s after the United States stopped allowing unrestricted imports of Kenyan fabrics—there were fears

Working Under the Hot Sun

There are not enough jobs to go around in the towns and cities. Between 35 and 50 percent of the people in urban areas are officially unemployed, but there is no welfare system to hand out benefits. Kenyans have always been inventive in setting up their own support groups, such as cooperatives. Today people have turned to creating their own job opportunities. They may be working in unregistered jobs, running their own street stand or restaurant, making pots and pans in a small business, driving a *matatu* (a type of taxi), shoe shining, or changing money for tourists. Factories are small, making goods such as tires, beer, chocolates, textiles, and plastic products. There are also self-employed craftsmen who work by the side of the road, hammering scrap metal into boxes, buckets, or charcoal-burning stoves. This informal sector is called *jua kali*, "hot sun" in Swahili, after the difficult conditions under which most people operate. They might be harassed by officials for not paying taxes, or have their goods confiscated or destroyed by the police. Yet *jua kali* is an important sector of the economy, accounting for 98 percent of all businesses in the country and growing at a much faster rate than the formal business sector. Programs have been set up to give these *jua kali* independent workers access to advice, training, and loans in the hope that many will turn into formal, tax-paying businesses.

that non-Kenyans were using the country as a cheap import route to the States. Cement production, once one of Kenya's most successful industries, has suffered from the irregular supply of raw material and the drop in value of the U.S. dollar (cement is valued in dollars). Steel-making is a growing industry.

Minerals and Mining

The bed of Lake Magadi in southern Kenya is almost entirely made of soda, which dyes the water a spectrum of colors, including vivid pink. Soda, Kenya's chief mineral export, is extracted from a crust, which forms on the surface of the lake. It is used to make washing soda, baking soda, glass, soap, and paper. Fluorite, a mineral used to make glass, enamel, and jewelry, and in met-alworking, is the next most important mineral. Sands containing millions of dollars worth of titanium and zirconium deposits were discovered around Mombasa in 1997 but they have yet to be mined. Gold, salt, and limestone are already being mined. Small-scale miners produce 20 percent of Kenya's gold. Limestone quarried in Kenya is used to make cement. Building stones are cut from exposed coral reefs. Kenya also has small deposits of semiprecious stones, including one called tsavorite, a rare green garnet discovered in Tsavo in 1971. Rubies of up to 66 pounds (30 kg) have been mined in Rift Valley Province. Mining still only accounts for 0.2 percent of Kenya's GDP (Gross Domestic Product).

The pink waters of Lake Magadi are the world's second-largest source of sodium carbonate (soda) after the Salton Sea in southeastern California. The soda is largely used in glassmaking.

Import Substitution

The government has long encouraged the manufacture of Kenyan-made goods. More recently, however, Kenya has made an effort to replace imported goods with Kenyan-made ones. To make their goods, though, many Kenyan manufacturers have to import the parts or raw materials, so trying to reduce imports —import substitution—has increased imports. Imported parts can be expensive, so it is difficult for Kenyan industries to produce goods at prices that will sell. To make it easier for manufacturers, the government has removed taxes on imports used by these industries. Export Processing Zones have been set up to help businesses produce goods for export.

Crafts such as basket weaving still provide work for many Kenyans.

Inflation, or rapidly rising prices, has been a severe problem in Kenya. In 1993 it soared to more than 60 percent. Prices rocketed for a variety of reasons: Foreign aid was suspended and price controls on imports were dropped in response to pressure from aid givers. Smaller but more expensive quantities of corn and other basic foodstuffs were produced after poor rains. By 1999 inflation had been brought back under control and was down to 6 percent.

Kenya is the world's third largest producer of sisal. This plant fiber is used to make textiles, ropes, twine, and baskets. Global sisal prices fell sharply in the 1990s, though, and the number of large sisal farms fell from more than 100 to fewer than 20.

Energy

Kenya uses its natural resources to supply about 25 percent of the energy people use. Hydroelectric plants on and around the Tana River use the rushing waters to generate electricity. A geothermal plant uses the hot natural springs of Lake Turkana to create power. Fossil fuels are also burned to make energy at an oil plant on the coast, but these fuels have to be imported since Kenya has no known large reserves of coal, oil, or natural gas. On the Kenyan side of the Kenya–Sudan border, the Elemi Triangle (*see* map p. 15) is believed to contain large deposits of petroleum. Both Kenya and Sudan claim the land as their own.

Kenya still has to import three-quarters of the energy it needs. A lot of hydroelectric energy is imported from Uganda, which has stations on the mighty Owen Falls, but this supply is becoming increasingly expensive. One as yet untapped source of renewable energy in Kenya is solar power.

TRANSPORTATION

Kenya has three international airports, one each at Mombasa, Nairobi, and Eldoret, President Moi's home town. The last was completed in 1996 at a cost of $49 million. People complained that it was a waste of money. The railroad has not been greatly extended since its creation, but it remains a vital route for the whole of eastern Africa and parts of central Africa. Kenya's road

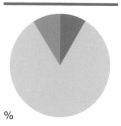

ENERGY SOURCES

%

- **83** Hydroelectric power
- **8** Fossil fuels (coal, gas, oil)
- **9** Other

Source: *CIA World Fact Book, 1998*

Kenya's few rivers produce a huge amount of hydroelectric power because of the many waterfalls in the country.

TRANSPORTATION

Kenya's comprehensive transportation system is one of the reasons for its economic importance in east Africa. The country's road network is concentrated around the hub of Nairobi and the towns of the Central Highlands. The main trunk route is the east-west road that links Mombasa with the towns of Lake Victoria. This is also the route of Kenya's main rail line. These links, together with the international airports at Mombasa and Nairobi, are almost as important for Kenya's neighbors as they are for Kenya itself.

- ——— Major highway
- ┼┼┼┼ Railroad
- ✈ Major airport
- ——— Navigable river

system is being renewed and extended, with major improvements planned to urban roads. This will benefit not just Kenyans but also nearby landlocked countries, such as Sudan, which need to send goods across Kenya to get to Mombasa.

TOURISM

In 1996 some 700,000 tourists brought $474 million into Kenya. Most tourists come from Germany, the United Kingdom, and Tanzania.

The main tourist areas are the coast, Nairobi, the Central Highlands, and nature parks such as Maasai Mara. Recent years have seen a decline in the number of visitors, perhaps put off by reports of "ethnic clashes" (*see* p. 118). Before the 1980s, most of the money in tourism was made by foreign investors and a few rich Kenyans. People like the Maasai profited little, even though they were sought out by tourists. As a result, some people have been hostile to tourism. Things have changed for some people since it was recognized that more Kenyans needed to be involved in the tourism business. The Maasai of Maasai Mara park, for example, now have a share in the money made from entrance fees and hotel bills. The funds go to two local councils who divide the money among the Maasai clans that own the land on the reserves.

INTERNATIONAL AID

Kenya first sought help from the International Monetary Fund (IMF) in the 1970s when money used to import goods far exceeded the amount Kenya earned from its exports. The cost of oil and other imports

The World Bank and the IMF

The World Bank was set up in 1945 to help Europe recover from the devastation left at the end of World War II. It still helps member nations develop economically and attempts to reduce poverty. Members have to first belong to the International Monetary Fund (IMF). The IMF was set up at the same time as the World Bank to foster international trade and financial cooperation, and often makes loans to member countries. The United States, Germany, France, China, Russia, Saudi Arabia, the United Kingdom, and Japan each appoints one of the 24 directors; the rest are elected by groups of other member nations.

Many countries accuse the World Bank and IMF of being controlled by rich countries for their own benefit. While African countries like Kenya are being forced to allow more foreign imports, rich countries discourage imports by setting quotas (limits) and tariffs (taxes). Kenya's external debt is still felt to be small by international standards. Representatives of poorer nations complain that they are not involved in policy making. At meetings of the World Bank in Seattle and Prague in 2000, many people protested against the bank's powers, drawing attention to the problems of poorer countries.

had risen sharply in that decade. Kenya has since received aid in the form of millions of dollars of grants and loans, but with strings attached. In 1997 the annual total was $457 million. Most of the conditions are economic: The government must cut costs, allow more imports, and reduce the value of the shilling. Import substitution policies were one of the conditions of aid set by the World Bank and the IMF. The Kenyan government finds it hard to balance donors' demands for strict belt-tightening in the economy with their citizens' demands for greater investment in schools, hospitals, and the environment.

In recent years, donors have helped pressure Moi into introducing multiparty democracy; aid has repeatedly been cancelled until reforms are made. Aid was recently withheld because of concerns about the government's human rights record and corruption. However, assistance to Kenya continues because the country is seen as a source of stability in an otherwise politically unstable region.

MAIN FOREIGN ARRIVALS

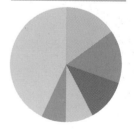

%

15   Germany

15   United Kingdom

12   Tanzania

8   Uganda

7   United States

43   Others

Source: Government of Kenya, 1997

Arts and Living

"An African is born into a community, a clan, and an age-group, not just a family"

Octavian Gakuru, senior Lecturer in Sociology, Nairobi University

Kenya is home to many vibrant cultures. Each ethnic group has its own unique art forms, dancing, music, and religion. These cultures are not rigid, however, but are dynamic, constantly changing and reforming, looking both to the past and to the future. To a certain extent, ethnic groups can be associated with a particular way of life. For example, the vast majority of Kikuyu people make their living from the land as farmers, while Maasai people are most likely to be animal herders. There are also many people from all ethnic groups who work in offices, schools, factories, and businesses.

ARTS

Art plays a central role in Kenyan society and history, being much more than the vision of just one person. Anyone can be involved in the production of art in a society, for example, where the human body itself is the canvas. The arts that Kenyan peoples have created serve many purposes, not only are they usually very pleasing to the eye, most have important social or political roles as well: The Mijikenda people who inhabit the lands along the coast used to mark their graves with richly carved wooden poles. These so-called funerary posts honor the dead, remind people of the values of Mijikenda society, and assert the authority of the elders. Maasai men would take hours to painstakingly style a friend's hair, and the

Although much of it follows traditional designs, Kenyan beadwork incorporates modern materials and is part of a culture that is constantly changing.

FACT FILE

● Kenya has four universities: Nairobi, Kenyatta (in Nairobi), Egerton (in Nakuru), and Moi (in Eldoret). There are around 35,000 students enrolled.

● The Meru people of northeast Kenya bless their newborn children by holding them up to Mount Kenya and wetting the child's face.

● In 1980, the government, concerned about the decline in Kenyan music, stated that 75 percent of the music played on Kenyan radio should be in Swahili and of Kenyan origin. However, the policy did not last.

A woodcarver works on a piece to be sold to tourists at Nanyuki near Mount Kenya.

end result would indicate the man's position in his community. Commonly, for example, many tiny braids caked with ocher, a pigment made from red clay, was the style of the youngest age group of adult Maasai men, the *moran*. Young friends may spend hours creating these designs for each other.

Among the nomads and seminomads of the drier regions of Kenya, the main art forms have often been portable ones that people can easily travel with. They have included beautifully designed shields, wooden headrests, jewelry, and the decoration of the human body. Personal, or body, art

Different Strokes

Among some of the peoples of Kenya specific crafts were traditionally despised. This goes back to the distinction between pastoralists, who lived off animals, and farmers, who lived off crops. Farmers developed crafts like weaving, metalwork, and leatherwork, which nomads considered beneath them, associating these crafts with the "settled" life of the farmers. Certain trades and crafts became associated with a specific minority group. This characteristic of Kenyan society is seen in the way that historically ethnic groups have tended to specialize in certain areas, for example, with the Kamba specializing in wood carving (*see* opposite).

is new to many in the West but it has a long history in Kenya, particularly among the Maasai, Turkana, and Samburu people.

Wood Carving

Although many no longer dress their hair and paint their bodies elaborately, Kenyan pastoralists are among the remaining few peoples who still use carved wooden headrests. Similar to those used in ancient Egypt thousands of years ago, they serve as both pillows and stools. A headrest would allow a man to protect his hairstyle while he slept: The rest would be positioned under one ear and along the side of the chin, leaving the hair untouched. Women pastoralists generally keep their hair short or shaved so they do not need to use headrests. Maasai, Somali, Turkana, and Samburu people all use headrests.

Wood carving is generally seen as man's work. Among the Turkana, however, women also carve wood, producing a variety of vessels for storage and display. The Kamba have a rich tradition of wood carving, and they are the main carvers for the tourist market in Kenya. The Kamba are famous for their slender, sticklike figures.

Beadwork

Pastoralist women dominate the production of beadwork. Among the Maasai, the men once produced most of the jewelry by metalworking. They made coiled iron bracelets to adorn the arms of married women and, later, brass charms, earrings, and necklaces. By the start of the 20th

Funerary posts, such as those below were produced by people living along Kenya's coast and were intended to remind the living of their obligations to respect the dead.

A young Somali woman living in a settlement of nomads in northern Kenya wears a fabric printed with a modern design.

century, however, mass-produced glass beads were imported into Kenya in quantity. Maasai women got hold of these beads through trade and started to make their own jewelry. Soon, they had taken over this valued role in Maasai society. Women continue to create and experiment with new forms: colorful plastic beads have replaced glass ones, while zippers, bottle tops, and even metal keys are worked into modern designs (*see* image p.92). Great attention is paid to the arrangement of colors to make the end result of the jewelry as eye-catching as possible. Contrasting colors are used to break up larger blocks of color.

Modern Arts in Kenya

Artists in Kenya who do not want to sell to the tourist market have a difficult time finding people to pay for their work. Government support for the arts has been sparse. Apart from the handful of active galleries and cultural centers in Nairobi, exhibition sites in Kenya are few. Despite these difficulties, Kenya has still produced many artists who have experimented with new forms and media, often in surprising and unusual ways. Sign-painting is a thriving business in Kenya, and several successful sign-painters create imaginative work that is far more sophisticated than the name suggests, often commenting on modern Kenyan society.

Pottery as Art

Many Kenyan women still mold and fire their own pots for domestic and household goods. Even pots that are to be used as simple containers are often pleasingly decorated and elegantly shaped. The increasing availability of cheap plastic and metal imported pots has not completely wiped this practice out. Some women have turned to making pots for the tourist market (*see* below).

One Kenyan-born potter, Magdalena Odundu (born 1950), has turned pottery into an artform. Odundu makes beautiful ceramic pottery that she has exhibited in Europe, the United States, and Asia.

Although based in Europe today, she studied art in Kenya and Nigeria. In her work she draws and builds on pottery techniques from cultures all over the world, both ancient and modern, to create pots that are unique and visually stunning. Like many African potters, she does not use a potter's wheel but shapes her pots by hand alone. She has described her work as "capturing the unfurling of a plant, the fall of a Victorian sleeve, the momentary stillness of a dancer's pose, or the silhouette of a Kenyan woman bound in layers of cloth."

Soapstone Carving

The Kisii (Gusii) people of Kenya are famous for their soapstone sculptures, which are in great demand at tourist markets in Nairobi, Mombasa, and elsewhere. The only other people in the world who produce soapstone carvings as part of such a large commercial venture are the Inuit of Québec, Canada. Soapstone, or steatite, is very compressed talc. It gets its name for its slightly greasy feel and because it was once used as soap. Among the Kisii, soapstone carving is a modern art

form, since it did not grow out of an older tradition. Although most of the carvings are sold to tourists, this does not detract from their value nor from the creativity of the artists. Indeed this is the only market where artists can sell their work. Wild animals, scenes of daily life, especially women at work and mother-and-child figures, are popular themes. Some sculptors have become famous for their more abstract sculptures.

Soapstone models of animals on sale in a hotel garden in Thika, near Mount Kenya.

MUSIC

Besides providing entertainment, songs could accompany workers in the field to keep their spirits up, keep herders company as they wiled away long hours alone, and celebrate special events such as weddings. Musical instruments typical of Kenya include horns made from the horns of kudu antelopes, bells, rattles, stringed instruments, and drums. One type of stringed instrument, the *nyatiti*, is typical of the Luo people. These double-necked stringed lyres have a skin cover that vibrates to amplify the sounds. The musician strikes one neck with a metal ring tied to his toe. The Borana, an Oromo-speaking people, and other pastoralists have created instruments from everyday household items. Being nomadic, this means their animals are not weighed down with excess baggage when on the move. The Borana's version of the guitar is called the cha-monge and is made from cooking pots strung with wires. Listeners have described Borana music as sounding like early blues music.

Maasai musical performances rely on no other instruments than the human voice and, at certain cere-monies, a kudu horn. Generally men sing together, standing in a line or semicircle. Each singer creates his own rhythm, over which a leader will sing short phrases. Dancing typically involved the men jumping high into the air from the same spot. Kamba dancers, who come from the region east and southeast of

Chuka dancers from the eastern side of Mount Kenya. Chuka music has now virtually died out, but the few remaining bands with their virtuoso drumming are justifiably famous.

Ngoma is a Bantu word for "drum" used in many African languages. In Kenya, it has also come to refer to drumming music played for people to dance to at social events as well as the act of dancing itself.

Nairobi, are famed for their spectacular acrobatic leaps, accompanied by drumming. They have a large repertoire of different types of songs, used for different occasions, but only a few of these are still sung today.

Pop Music

Gospel music has displaced many Kenyan dancing and music traditions, and pop music is more popular with many young people than the songs and dances their grandparents more regularly performed.

Nairobi is the heart of east Africa's popular music scene. Musicians from all over east and central Africa perform there. Guitar bands were all the rage in the first half of the 20th century, and by the 1950s, *benga* music had evolved. Originally a Luo creation, *benga* has since spread throughout Kenya. *Benga* uses guitars, electric ones today, to create music based on the fast beats of Luo *ngoma* and the sound of instruments such as the *nyattiti* and *orutu*, a one-stringed fiddle. Hundreds of *benga* bands were performing in the 1970s, and the style has influenced Kenyan pop ever since. Most groups sing in Kenyan languages, not English, and Swahili-language groups have universal appeal. Women play a big role in Kikuyu pop groups, as both lead and backing singers. Some Kenyan songwriters make brave attempts with their lyrics to address political and social issues, despite the risk of arrest.

Them Mushrooms

On Kenya's coast there is a lively music scene that caters largely to the tourist trade. Many groups of musicians manage to make a living simply from playing at the hotels. These groups mix Congolese rhythms with cover versions of international songs. For the last 30 years the most successful of these bands has been Them Mushrooms. They began as a reggae band working the hotel circuit and moved to Nairobi in 1987. Their most successful song is *"Jambo Bwana."* Its famous refrain *Hakuna Matata,* which means "No Problems, No Worries," was a reassuring slogan in Kenya in the 1970s, when there was considerable unrest in countries surrounding Kenya. The refrain is heard in the title song of the 1994 Disney movie *The Lion King.* Today the group has recorded more than 15 albums and has had many successful collaborations with other Kenyan artists.

Festival Music

On Kenya's islands and along the coast, *taarab* music is played at parties, weddings, homes, and funerals, in clubs and restaurants, and on the radio. Widely distributed throughout Kenya on tapes, *taarab* remains distinctly coastal. Like the Swahili people themselves, it is African in its roots with Arabic and Indian influences. The word *taarab* comes from the Arabic for "to be moved or shook up" and is also the name of an African drum, the *tarabu*. In Swahili, it is used to refer to the event as well as the music, so friends will ask each other if they are going to the *taarab* tonight. Melodies often copy those made popular by the latest movie hit from Bollywood (Bombay), the Indian movie capital. The style of singing is directly descended from ancient Swahili poetry, which was performed by singers to the sound of drums and stringed instruments.

Taarab music continues to evolve, and today stringed instruments are generally electronic. Percussion is a crucial element of the music, and every band will have at least three drummers, playing rhythms based on local *ngoma* (drumming). *Taarab* bands are in great demand for the week-long Swahili weddings. Men and women generally party separately, and the women make up songs on the spot to tease and advise the new bride. Guests pass money to the singer to request a song, or show approval of particular lyrics, and everyone dances the *chakacha*: a vigorous swaying dance. Ancient Swahili poems, some written by women, once lectured newly wed women on how to please their husbands. At a wedding party today, *taarab* lyrics are just as likely to be advice on how to stand up to a husband!

Swahili Architecture

From at least the 1200s, Swahili stone houses have been a feature of the Kenyan coast. In Mombasa, Lamu, Pate, and other historic coastal towns some people

Carved wooden doors, such as this example from Lamu island are typical of Swahili architecture.

still live in stone houses remarkably similar to those known only as ruins today. Although few houses in these ports were built before the 20th century, they look much older because people have kept building and rebuilding in the same style.

At first, only the most wealthy families in a town could afford to build a stone house. As more and more people prospered from trade, however, more stone houses were built. By the 1700s, most people in Lamu, for instance, lived in stone houses. One family would occupy a whole block, or *mtaa*, of linked houses. The houses were arranged so that female residents could lead their lives in private, visiting nearby relatives and friends without walking the streets. Instead, they used connecting bridges and internal passages. The wife of a wealthy Muslim was not usually seen in public.

The entrance to the house is normally a porch that leads to an internal courtyard, the main focus of the house. Two or three stories of living rooms overlook the courtyard, with openings in the walls for doors and to admit light. The houses have long, narrow rooms because short mangrove poles were originally used as roof beams. Niches (*zidaka*) of different depths and slants set into the walls gave the rooms the illusion of space, by making the walls look farther away than they were. In the past, brass lamps, Chinese pottery, and other foreign artifacts would be displayed in the niches.

The women's living quarters, generally at the secluded rear of the house, are often better decorated than all the others and are kept private by a single entrance door. Privacy was an important element to the architects who designed these houses and to the people who lived in them. Visitors should not be able to glance into the women's quarters, so the position of doors was carefully planned to avoid this happening. These considerations allow residents and guests to mingle together without losing too much privacy, so there would be a distinction between areas used by the family alone and others used for social purposes. Houses are not just for the family's use: People get married there in ceremonies that last for days, with the central courtyard and sumptuous living rooms providing a perfect backdrop to the ceremony.

In addition to domestic Swahili architecture, there are a number of forts along Kenya's coastline. Perhaps most striking of these is the vast Siyu fort on Pate Island (*see* below). Siyu was once a center of Islamic scholarship, virtually untouched by the Portuguese and a haven for skilled workmanship such as Koran-copying, leatherwork, bookmaking, and carving. At its peak the town of Siyu was home to 4,000 people. The fort went into decline after it was occupied by the Omani sultan of Zanzibar in 1847, although today it has been extensively renovated.

ATHLETICS

In the last 20 years Kenya has gained a reputation as perhaps the strongest distance-running team in the world. Athletes train in camps at high-altitude in the Central Highlands of the country. At high altitude there is less oxygen in the air and so conditions mimic the experience of oxygen depletion a runner will undergo during a distance race. Because conditions are quite basic, relatively few foreigners come to train at the camps, so a tight-knit community is formed among the Kenyan athletes. This means that in races they often set the pace for each other, running as a team rather than as individuals. The strategy has definitely paid off. Kenyan athletes have achieved success in both the Olympics and the Athletics World Championships at 800 m, 1500 m, 3,000 m, 10,000 m, and the marathon.

Kenya's Noah Ngeny crosses the finish line to win the gold in the Men's 1500 m at the Sydney 2000 Olympics. He is followed by El Gerrouj of Morocco, third is Kenya's Baernard Lagat.

DAILY LIFE

For rural Kenyans, daily life is centered around the land: tending crops and looking after animals. While not all families have someone who earns a wage, the whole family still has plenty of chores to do. Members of the same community will help each other out when times are hard. A lot of the crops grown for food rather than sale are farmed by women. Men prefer the more profitable cash crops or animal herding. Besides keeping up with their schoolwork, children, especially girls, might have to help with collecting firewood, fetching water, and preparing meals. Boys might be responsible for looking after the animals.

Very few Kenyans today have electricity or running water in their homes. Women or girls can spend hours each day walking to the local water supply or their nearest wooded area to collect enough water or wood for their cooking fires. Limited by what they can carry on foot, the same journey may have to be made each day. It need not always be like this, though. Women's groups working with the government and aid agencies have developed stoves that use less fuel than a typical fire, and solar-powered ovens are being developed in Kenya that could be made by people at home.

Cooperatives, such as this rice-planting program near Machakos, work with the government to provide local employment.

Public Holidays

January 1	New Year's Day
May 1	Labor Day
June 1	Madaraka Day: the anniversary of self-government in Kenya, two years before full independence.
October 10	Moi Day: the anniversary of President Moi becoming president.
October 20	Kenyatta Day: the anniversary of Jomo Kenyatta's arrest by colonialists.
December 12	Jamhuri Day: the anniversary of Kenya's full independence from Britain.
December 25	Christmas Day
December 26	Boxing Day
March—April	Good Friday and Easter Monday
December—February (dates vary)	Eid-al-Fitr: the Muslim celebration of the end of the holy month of Ramadan. Ramadan is believed to be the time when the Koran, the Muslim holy book, was handed down by Allah (God) to the Prophet Muhammad.

The Samburu, who live north of Mount Kenya, are closely related to the Maasai. From adolescence to their 30s men are warriors and hunters; they then become elders and are free to marry. The Samburu live in mud huts and keep some livestock for milk.

On the Move

Among the pastoralists, such as the Maasai, Rendille, Samburu, and Turkana people, life is very different from that of the settled farmers. Most are nomads or seminomads who move from place to place with their animals as the seasons change. When the rains come in Kenya, dry, barren grasslands are transformed into lush green pastures—only for a while, though, since the rainy season does not last long over much of the savannas. If people remained in one place, their animals would soon starve or die of thirst. Young Maasai men might spend many months away from their main home during the dry season, looking after their family's herds at a distant watering hole. The drier the land is, the more often people have to move. So in the far north of Kenya many Somali, Oromo, and Turkana people have

The Pros and Cons of Change

In some savanna areas boreholes have been drilled and fitted with wind-driven pumps to raise underground water to the surface. While this has improved the lives of many Kenyans, it has had some side effects. Year-round access to water has allowed people to settle more permanently in one place and keep larger herds. Better access to veterinary care has also allowed herd sizes to grow. This can lead to overgrazing and, in severe cases, desertification: Tropical soils are fragile and only a thin top layer is fertile. Grasslands not given time to recover from trampling and grazing lose their fertility and can become barren, desertlike plains. At times of poor rainfall, some pastoralists in Kenya are in greater danger today of starvation than they were in their less-settled past. After a lack of rainfall in the 1990s, famine was only prevented in some areas by the distribution of food by aid agencies.

Yet pastoralists were once able to cope with the droughts. In the past they might have moved on, spread out over a wider area, or stocked up on hardier animals such as goats and sheep. Many of these options are no longer possible. Since British rule, governments have encouraged nomads to settle in one place, making them easier to tax and control. Pastoralists have lost much of their historic pasture lands to settlers, neighboring countries, farmers, and even as land set aside for national parks.

*A Samburu family
outside their
traditional home,
made of woven
branches and
plastered in mud.*

to travel even more than the Maasai. They often keep more camels than cattle, since these animals can survive long periods without water. The camels can be loaded up with all a family's possessions as they move from water-hole to waterhole. The Turkana of northern Kenya might take their animals to the lush Rift Valley floor in the wet season. In the dry season, the cattle and sheep are taken to the cooler mountains, while the hardier camels and goats stay to browse the shrubs that survive the lack of rain.

HOME LIFE

Most rural Kenyans now live in houses made of cement blocks, with corrugated metal roofs. In the cities and towns, concrete and brick are the preferred building materials. Along the coasts, houses made from coral stone are also common. The stone is mined from reefs that have been left exposed by a changing coastline.

As they become increasingly settled, the Maasai are spending more and more time in what were once homes

The local cuisine of Mombasa is based on smoked fish and fresh vegetables.

just used in the rainy season. Built by women, they were made of cattle manure, mud, and grass. To make them durable, a thin waterproof coating of cement on the roof and gutters to channel off rainwater are now being added.

Dinner Time

At meal times, a family will eat together, often sharing food from the same dishes. Typical Kenyan meals are best eaten with the fingers, but food is served from the main bowls with spoons. Instead of plates, dinner might be served in calabashes, which are dried, hollowed-out gourds. Calabashes, decorated with bold or intricate patterns burned into them are kept for special meals. Kenyan food includes *ugali*, a dish made from corn that is similar to American grits, Indian flat chapati breads and three-cornered pastries called samosas, and stews. *Nyama choma* (beef roasted

Goods Ownership

Ownership of consumer goods in Kenya is extremely low among the general population. The country has 730,000 TV sets and 290,000 telephones, about one telephone for every 100 people. Automobile ownership is also low, with about one vehicle for every 100 people. These statistics are deceptive, however, because there are great variations within the country. Many rural peoples live without any contact with modern appliances, while people living in cities such as Nairobi may have contact with modern technology not dissimilar from people in any other modern city. The small market for modern technology means that little in the way of consumer goods are made in Kenya. Those on sale in the shops are mainly imported, creating problems for the country's trade balance.

Nyama Choma

Nyama choma is a meat stew cooked with vegetables. In Kenya people use many different kinds of meat, and you can vary the type of meat you use according to your taste.

You will need:

3 lbs beef (chuck or brisket cut into pieces for stew)

2 or 3 ripe tomatoes

1 onion, sliced

1 cup soaked, cooked beans

2 cloves of garlic, crushed

½ cup red wine vinegar

1 cup water

½ tsp. turmeric

½ tsp. ginger

½ tsp. cinnamon

Salt and pepper to taste

Method:

Place all the ingredients in an ovenproof casserole dish with a tight-fitting lid. Cover and bake in a 375°F oven for 2–3 hours. The dish can be made a day in advance so that the flavors have a chance to mix. This creates a richer-tasting stew.

over a fire or stewed in a casserole) and *irio*, a thick sauce made with peas, corn, spices, and potatoes, are also favorite dishes. *Ugali* is cooked in boiling water until it has the same consistency and texture as bread dough, then eaten with sauces or stews. *Sukuma wiki* is a leaf in the kale family that appears in many Kenyan dishes. Bananas cooked in banana leaves are a treat in western and central Kenya. Goat and beef are the most popular meats throughout the country.

Families, Age Sets, and Clans

Kenyans are very aware that they do not belong to just a family but to larger social groups as well. These other groups can include age sets, homesteads, and clans. Several Kikuyu family groups (*nyumba*), not necessarily related, may live together in homesteads (*mucii*). The

Pokot boys during an initiation ceremony. The Pokot are part of the Kalenjin language group and are pastoralists who inhabit the scrubland north of Lake Baringo.

members of a *mucii* live and work together for everyone's benefit. In the past, several *mucii* formed a *mbari*, which in turn made up the ten clans of the Kikuyu. Among the Maasai the *enkang* is the next unit up from the family. Like the Kikuyu homestead, it is made up of several families living and working together. Several *enkang* would make up a clan.

Many Kenyans belong to a particular age set, which is made up of girls or boys who are initiated at the same time. Initiation is an important ceremony that transforms a girl into a woman and a boy into a man. The members of an age set, like a class at school, move up through the various age grades together. The highest age grade is that of elder. The elders of the community were historically its leaders. They would debate important issues facing the community and decide together how to deal with them. Elders are still highly respected but, like the clans, they have lost most of their political powers to politicians. Among the Maasai, newly initiated young men belong to the *moran* age grade. Historically, *moran* would have defended their community and perhaps gone on cattle raids when times were bad. For this reason they have been called warriors, which at times they were, but their responsibilities also included looking after their clan's herds.

GOING TO SCHOOL

Kenyans recognize the value of a good education, and both the government and individual parents have invested heavily in building schools. A lot of schools were set up by parents many years ago when Kenya was a British colony. Denied access to the white-only schools, Kenyans got together and literally built their own. This became a tradition that has continued with the building of *harambee* schools (*see* p. 70) since independence. Today, the government runs many schools and provides training and financial help to *harambee* schools.

Primary school education, from the age of 6 to 14, is compulsory and free of charge in Kenya. Around 85 percent of children attend. Attendance is highest in the cities. Children go to secondary school from the age of 14 to 18. There are not enough places for everyone, however, and many schools charge fees that most parents cannot afford to pay. As a result, less than 30 percent of children attend secondary schools.

ATTENDANCE AT SCHOOL

Higher	2%
Secondary	24%
Primary	85%

Limited places in government-built secondary schools mean that many pupils are educated in community-built harambee *schools.*

Literature

Storytelling, poetry, and song have long been vehicles for Kenyan culture. Legends, histories, and old and new stories are re-told or sung at social events and at cere-monies. In the 20th century, Kenyans in the area west of the coast began to write their stories down and publish them for the first time. A significant body of written literature soon emerged. The injustices of the colonial era inspired many books, which in turn lead to many arrests, and this tradition of political writing continues to the present day. The most famous Kenyan writer is Ngugi wa Thiong'o (born 1938). His novels, poems, plays, and academic works have been published and performed all over the world. He began his career writing in English but switched to writing in Kikuyu since he believes that African literature should cater to African readers, rather than readers in the United States and Europe. After being arrested for his writings in 1976, he was released two years later, but left Kenya in 1982 for the U.S., where he lives in exile.

Kenya has 15 doctors and 23 qualified nurses for every 100,000 people—an extremely low rate. Private healthcare is mainly run by charities and religious missions.

HEALTH CARE

Since independence a vast vaccination program, partly funded by the World Health Organization, and nation-ally-funded improvements in education, sanitation, and nutrition have drastically reduced the death rate in Kenya. Problems still exist, however, especially diseases associated with a lack of clean drinking water, such as dysentery. Malaria is also common in the area around Lake Victoria in western Kenya. Among pastoralists of the arid northern areas herbal and other locally-pro-duced forms of medicine combat disease.

The greatest health problem facing Kenya today is AIDS. Thirty-four million people in sub-Saharan Africa are carriers of the disease and 50 percent of hospital cases in Kenya are HIV-related. Most people in Kenya cannot afford the life-prolonging drugs that are avail-able to people in wealthier countries. Those affected are often young adults and there are fears that the disease will create labor shortages in Kenya's already over-stretched health service. The gloomiest predictions are of a million orphans left dependent on the state.

RELIGION

There is no official state religion in Kenya, but more than three-quarters of Kenyans are Christian. Less than 10 percent are Muslim and less than 1 percent are Hindu. The constitution enshrines freedom of religion in law, and the government generally respects this. Most Kenyans today are tolerant of the religions of others, and one street may even boast a church, a mosque, and a temple.

Christianity was originally introduced to Kenya by Europeans, but today most Kenyan Christians belong to independent African churches. The churches may be small, founded and run by a local minister, or large, with converts from many regions. Many Kenyans combine their faith with elements from their ancestors'

The richly decorated entrance to the Sikh temple in central Mombasa.

Myths and Legends

Each of Kenya's peoples have their own myths and legends, often including some that link the people to their ancestral homelands. For the Kikuyu, for example, Mount Kenya is very symbolic. It is said to be the home of the all-powerful god, Ngai. According to legend, the Kikuyu are descended from Gikuyu, one of Ngai's three sons. Gikuyu was given the fertile lands of central Kenya to farm and a wife called Mumbi. Mumbi gave birth to nine daughters, who are the origin of the nine of the ten main clans of the Kikuyu today. This mountain is called *Keré Nyaga* (Mountain of Mystery, or Whiteness) by Kikuyu people. The tenth Kikuyu clan has a separate, more recent origin.

religions, elements which are not necessarily contradictory to Christianity. This has led to a uniquely African form of Christianity. Common to many African religions is the showing of respect for dead ancestors, who are seen as links with the other world. They are often remembered and turned to for advice or help by relatives who may donate gifts to a good cause in their name or make offerings of food directly to them.

El Molo people leaving a mission church in northern Kenya.

African Religions

The Turkana and the Maasai still largely follow their own religions. Akuj is the Turkana god, and he is believed to be responsible for providing or withholding rain. He is rarely addressed directly, but instead through ancestors or "dreamers," men chosen by Akuj to act as his messengers to the people. The Maasai god is called Ngai, which also means sky. Ngai is referred to as both "he" and "she," and was originally one with the earth, but then earth and Ngai separated. Ngai created all the cattle on earth for the Maasai. Religious leaders called *laibons* once played important social roles in Maasai society, predicting the future, giving advice, healing, and directing rituals and ceremonies. Today, their political roles lost to local officials, they more often offer their services to individual clients than the whole community. Maasai *laibons* are in demand for their reputation as natural healers. They have an extensive knowledge of plants and their medicinal uses, and other Kenyans see them as people who have not forgotten their past knowledge.

Speaking Swahili

Swahili is one of the Bantu languages and emerged on the coast of east Africa. Bantu languages have been spoken along the east African coast since the first millennium A.D. However, Swahili was also influenced by several other languages, such as Arabic, Persian, Hindi, Portuguese, and English. These borrowings occurred because of the history of trade along east Africa's coast. Merchants and sailors exchanged words from different languages, developing a spoken language which developed into the Swahili that exists today. Modern Swahili often includes terms that are recognizable as coming from other languages, such as the Portuguese *vino* for "wine" and *baisikeli* for "bicycle." Spelling of Swahili words is still not standardized throughout Kenya. The standard dialect is derived from Zanzibar Swahili, which was the version learned by the early missionaries.

Swahili vowels are short and always pronounced, even when next to another vowel. So *mzee* (elder) sounds like "mm-zey-ey." Consonants in Swahili are generally pronounced as in English, with a few differences. Here are some useful words and phrases in Swahili:

Please	*Tafadhali* (Taf-aDAR-lee)
Thank you	*Asante (ah-SAN-tay)*
Yes	*Ndiyo (ndEE-yo)*
No	*Hapana (ha-PAR-nah)*
Hello	*Jambo* or *Salamba* (YAM-bo/sa-LAM-bah)
Goodbye	*Kwaheri (kwah-ER-ee)*
How are you?	*Habari? (ha-BAR-ee)*
I'm fine thanks	*Nzuri (nZUR-ee)*
What's your name?	*Unaitwa nani?* (oon-AEET-wa NAHnee)
My name is...	*Jina langu ni...* (JEE-na-LAHN-goo-nee)

Numbers:

One	*Moja (MOH-ja)*
Two	*Mbili (mBEE-lee)*
Three	*Tatu (TAH-too)*
Four	*Nne (NAY)*
Five	*Tano (TAH-noh)*
Six	*Sita (SEET-ah)*
Seven	*Saba (SAH-ba)*
Eight	*Nane (NAH-nay)*
Nine	*Tisa (TEE-sah)*
Ten	*Kumi (KOO-mee)*

Days of the week:

Sunday	*Jumapili (JOO-mah-pee-lee)*
Monday	*Jumatatu (JOO-ma-too-too)*
Tuesday	*Jumanne (JOO-mah-nay)*
Wednesday	*Jumatano* (JOO-mah-tarn-OO)
Thursday	*Alhamisi (al-ha-MEE-see)*
Friday	*Ijumaa (ee-JOO-mah)*
Saturday	*Jumamosi (JOO-mah-MOH-see)*

The Future

*"May our society be cream, may it be milk,
may it be honey and beer."*

Maasai prayer

After many years of struggle, Kenya has returned to multiparty politics. Kenyans are still campaigning hard to ensure that things continue to improve. People such as ecologist Wangari Maathai and political activist Koigi wa Wamere have risked their lives for the future of their country. They, and others, have been arrested, detained, and beaten for their efforts. Kenyans still want to decrease the powers of the president and weed out corrupt officials. Not convinced that the government is sincere about reforms, churches, charities, opposition politicians, and members of the public have decided to conduct their own constitutional review, but opposition meetings and rallies are still being disrupted by police or state-sponsored gangs.

Battling Poverty

Economically, Kenya has great promise but much poverty. More than 50 percent of Kenyans live on less than $1 per day. Working toward the goal of bringing poverty to an end, self-help movements continue to flourish. They are perhaps the greatest hope for Kenya's future. *Harambee* movements, cooperatives, women's groups such as Maendeleo ya Wanawake Organization (MYWO, "Women's Progress"), and anyone working in business, including the *jua kali* (*see* p. 86), are doing their best to improve things for themselves.

Wildebeest roam across a field in front of the high-rises of Nairobi, a mix of traditional and modern images of Kenya.

FACT FILE

- Elections in 2002 will see the close of one period in Kenya's history, the Moi years, and the start of a new era.

- In 1975, radical politician J. M. Karuiki warned that Kenya could become a land of "ten million peasants and ten millionaires." Today, the richest 2 percent of the people consume nearly 35 percent of national income, and the poorest 60 percent less than 30 percent.

- In July 1999, Dr. Richard Leakey was appointed Secretary to the Cabinet, Head of the Civil Service, and Governor of the Central Bank with the task of cleaning up corruption in politics.

117

Plans are being made to resurrect the East African Community, which would help Kenya develop greater trade networks within Africa. This could decrease the economy's reliance on cheap exports of raw materials to the Western world and on aid.

Aid to Kenya

Much of Kenya's aid money is not given but loaned, and the Kenyan government repays a huge amount of money on its debts every year. This makes investment in roads, schools, hospitals, and industry difficult. International pressure has risen in recent years to cancel the debts of African countries, as has been done in Latin America. Germany has canceled Kenya's debt, on condition that more money is invested in the environment. Other creditors have agreed to lower interest rates. The World Bank and IMF, the two biggest donors and those that have the most control over Kenya's economy, have begun to respond to criticisms, though very slowly. The World Bank now makes economic policies that relieve poverty a condition of aid. It has been recognized that ignoring poverty only forces people to plunder their environment, putting Kenya's future in jeopardy.

Ethnic Conflict

The rebirth of multiparty politics has been stressful and has triggered the fear of widespread ethnic conflict in the near future. Moi used the threat of ethnic conflict to justify one-party rule for many years. He claimed that since most political parties draw their support from a particular ethnic group, political rivalries would become actual conflicts. When multiparty politics were introduced in 1992, more than 2,000 died and 20,000 were made homeless after violent attacks on people in western Kenya. In 1993, serious disorders broke out among the Maasai, Kikuyu, and Kalenjin, particularly in the Rift Valley area. Thousands of Kikuyus were driven from their homes, which were taken over mostly by Kalenjin. Revenge soon followed though. By 1994 more than 300,000 people had been displaced and at least 1,500 killed.

Described as "ethnic clashes" in press reports, the initial attacks seem to be unprovoked and more like military maneuvers than random clashes. Witnesses report seeing hundreds of young men, armed with bows and arrows and often dressed identically in shorts and T-shirts. Kenyan police and security forces have been accused of doing little to protect victims. The government has blamed the multiparty system for inciting ethnic clashes. Moi's critics, as well as international observers and human rights groups, have accused the government of being involved in stirring up the conflicts.

Many Kenyans are making great efforts to deal with these conflicts. Hope lies in the use of old-fashioned forms of conflict solving that some pastoralists have recently brought back with success. From 1992 to 1995, Wajir District in northern Kenya was a war zone. Drought had struck, and clans of Somali pastoralists were battling over grazing and water rights while refugees from the civil war in Somalia were pouring over the border. Local leaders, Somali elders, and government officials worked together to stop the fighting. By allowing the elders time to conduct their own peace meetings to handle crises, the conflict came to an end. Crucial to the agreement's success was its being sealed by the sacrifice of an animal, in the time-honored manner.

Some people are calling for Kenya to become a federal republic, made up of states each with its own government. This movement is called Majimboism. Other people fear this could make life difficult for the minority ethnic groups of each state and perhaps even bring conflict.

Voices from Kenya

Here are the views of some leading Kenyan thinkers on the issues that face Kenya at present and in the future:

Political scientist, Ali Mazrui: "Clearly Africa is not the nearest in culture to the Western world, yet the continent has indeed been experiencing perhaps the fastest pace of Westernization this century of anywhere in the non-Western world."

Wangari Maathai, ecologist, founder of the women's Green Belt Movement: "I am not opposed to development, but development that plunders resources like forests, land, air, and food, oblivious of the needs of tomorrow, is short-sighted and self-defeating."

Koigi wa Wamere, human rights activist, on trial for his life in Nairobi: "If we see evil and injustices but do nothing about them, they could last forever despite our knowledge of and hatred for them. When we see evil and injustices, we must expose and fight to end them."

Almanac

POLITICAL

Country name:
Official long form: Republic of Kenya
Conventional short form: Kenya

Nationality:
noun: Kenyan
adjective: Kenyan

Official languages: English and Swahili

Capital city: Nairobi

Type of government: republic

Suffrage (voting rights): 18 years
and over, universal

National anthem: "O God of
All Creation"

National holiday: Independence Day
December 12, 1963

Flag:

GEOGRAPHICAL

Location: Eastern Africa, bordering
the Indian Ocean, latitudes 5°
north to 5° south and
longitudes 34° to 42 ° east

Climate: Tropical on the coast and
in the far west and arid in the
interior. Temperate areas in
the Central Highlands.

Total area: 224,903 square miles
(582,650 sq. km)
land: 98%
water: 2%

Coastline: 333 miles (536 km)
Terrain: low plains rise to Central
Highlands bisected by Great Rift
Valley; fertile plateau in west
Highest point: Mount Kenya,
17,057 feet (5,199 m)
Lowest point: Coast of Indian Ocean,
0 feet
Natural resources: gold, limestone,
soda ash, salt barites, rubies,
fluorspar,. garnets
Land use: arable land 7%
forests and woodland 30%
permanent crops 1%
permanent pasture 37%
other: 25%

Natural hazards: recurring drought in northern and eastern regions; flooding during rainy seasons

POPULATION

Population: (2000 est.) 29 million

Population density: 132 people per square mile (51 per sq. km)

Population growth rate: 1.53%

Birthrate (2000 est.): 29.35 births per 1,000 of the population

Death rate (1999 est.): 14.08 deaths per 1,000 of the population

Sex ratio (1999 est.): 101 males per 100 females

Total fertility rate (1999 est.): 3.66 per woman in the population

Infant mortality rate (1999 est.): 68.74 deaths per 1,000 live births

Life expectancy at birth (1999 est.):
total population: 47.98 years
male: 46.95 years
female: 49.04 years
Literacy: (1990 est.)
total population: 78.1%
male: 86.3%
female: 70%

ECONOMY

Currency: 1 Kenyan shilling (Ksh);
= 100 cents
Exchange rate (1999):
$1 = Ksh 73.94

Gross national product (1997):
$9.7 billion (83rd-largest economy in the world)

Average annual growth rate (1990–1997): 2.1%

GNP per capita (1999 est.): $340

Average annual inflation rate (1990–1998): 18.1%

Unemployment rate (1997 est.): 35%

Exports (1997): $1.96 billion
Imports (1997): $3.28 billion

Foreign aid received (1996): $457 million

Human Development Index
(an index scaled from 0 to 100 combining statistics indicating adult literacy, years of schooling, life expectancy, and income levels):
46.3 (U.S. 94.3)

TIME LINE—KENYA

World History

Kenyan History

c. 50,000 B.C.

c. **40,000** Modern humans—*Homo sapiens sapiens*—emerge.

c. 3,000 B.C.

3000–1000 B.C. Height of ancient Egyptian civilization.

1200–1000 B.C. Phoenicians rise to power in the Mediterranean.

753 B.C. City of Rome founded.

332 B.C. Alexander the Great creates Greek empire.

c. **2000** B.C. Cushitic settlers move south into Kenya from Ethiopia.

c. **1000** B.C. Eastern Cushitics begin to occupy central Kenya.

c. **500** B.C.–A.D. **500** Other peoples settle in Kenya.

A.D. 0

c. A.D. **1** Birth of Jesus Christ.

A.D. **476** Goths sack Rome.

c. **570–632** Life of Prophet Mohammed.

1526 Foundation of Mughal empire in India.

1492 Christopher Columbus arrives in America.

1300-1600 Renaissance in Western Europe leads to the rebirth of classical learning.

1288 Ottoman state founded in Turkey.

1065 Start of the Crusades.

c. **1000** Vikings land in New-foundland but do not settle.

1600s Wanga kingdom founded.

1593 Construction of Fort Jesus.

1585 Ottoman Turks attack Portuguese settlements.

1528 Nuna de Cunha loots Mombasa.

1498 Vasco da Gama leads European exploration of east Africa.

1300

11th century Chinese expedition reaches east African coast.

c. **1000** Bantu-speaking peoples arrive from west Africa.

c. A.D. **700** Arab traders bring Islam to east Africa.

A.D. 700

1750

1776 American Declaration of Independence.

1750–1850 Industrial Revolution in the West.

1792–1815 Napoleonic Wars in Europe.

1822 Omani army sent to subdue Mombasa.

1846 First missionaries arrive in Mombasa.

2000 The West celebrates the Millennium— 2,000 years since the birth of Christ.

1999 Kosovo conflict in Europe.

1994 End of apartheid in South Africa.

1991 End of Cold War.

1990 Gulf War.

1998 Terrorist attack on U.S. embassy in Nairobi.

1997 Multiparty elections lead to reelection of Moi and ethnic violence.

1992 Increasing corruption leads to withdrawal of foreign aid.

1982 Kenya officially becomes a one-party state.

1978 Kenyatta succeeded by Daniel arap Moi.

1850

1888 Imperial British East Africa Company founded.

1890s Series of treaties with African peoples give British control of large areas of Kenya.

1895 Britain declares protectorate over Uganda and Kenya.

c. 1910 European settlers establish plantations.

1920 British East Africa becomes the colony Kenya.

1940s–1950s Mau Mau uprising.

1880s European "Scramble for Africa."

1914–1918 World War I.

1929 Wall Street Crash, beginning of Great Depression.

1933 Nazis come to power in Germany.

1939–1945 World War II.

1975

1973–1974 World Oil Crisis.

1969 First man lands on the moon.

1963–1975 Vietnam War.

1962 Cuban Missile Crisis.

1967 East African Trade Community declared.

1966 Kenya People's Union formed.

1963 Kenyan independence.

1952 State of Emergency.

1946 Kenyatta returns to Kenya.

1945

Glossary

Abbreviation: Sw. = Swahili

age sets: Groupings of people according to age, which hold different roles in society (warriors, elders, etc.).

Bantu: African people originating in west and central Africa who emigrated to southern and central Kenya from 500 B.C.
British East Africa: Area of east Africa controlled by the British, encompassing modern Kenya.

canopy: The part of a forest just beneath the uppermost leaves or branches.
capitalism: An economic system based on supply and demand, and private ownership of businesses and industry.
cash crops: Crops such as tea and coffee, grown not for domestic consumption, but for export in order to generate foreign currency.
Central Rift: Cavernous valley in central Kenya caused by a rupture in the earth's crust.
colonialism: Control of one country or people by another.
Cushites: People who migrated to northern and central Kenya from the Ethiopian Highlands in the second millennium B.C.

desertification: The process of becoming desertlike.
dhow: Sailing vessel, introduced to Kenya by the sailors of ancient Arabia.

export: A product that is sold to another country.

FORD: Forum for the Restoration of Democracy. Kenyan opposition party.

GDP (Gross Domestic Product): The total value of goods produced in a country during one year.

Harambee (Sw.): Community self-help and voluntary fundraising—a policy promoted by Kenyatta.
hominid: A family of early primates that included human ancestors.

import substitution: The attempt to replace goods bought from abroad with those produced domestically, in order to prevent a net outflow of wealth from a country.
infrastructure: The basic framework of public works, such as transportation, building, and public services.
Islam: Religion based on the teachings of Muhammad.

jua kali (Sw.): Literally "hot sun," small-scale, informal work usually performed out of doors.

Kikuyu: Kenya's largest ethnic group whose original heartland was the region surrounding Mount Kenya.
KANU: Kenyan African National Union, Kenya's ruling political party.

laibon (Sw.): Chief or spiritual leader of the Maasai.

Maasai: Hunter gatherer people who live on the Kenyan plains.
Mau Mau: Kenyan independence movement that employed terrorist methods against British colonials.
Muhammad: Seventh-century founder of the religion of Islam.
moorland: An area of open, uncultivated land.
moran (Sw.): Maasai or Samburu warrior.
mosque: The religious building of Islam.
Muslim: A follower of Islam.
mzee (Sw.): An older person or respected elder.

nationalization: The placing of private industry under government or public control.
Nilotes: People who emigrated to Kenya from the area of the Nile River in southern Sudan between 1000 B.C. and A.D. 1500.
ngoma (Sw.): A drum or more usually a type of music based on drumming.

Omani: Arab people from the east of the Arabian peninsula.

paleontology: The study of early geological periods

through fossil remains.
pastoralist: A person who lives by keeping livestock.

radical: A person seeking rapid changes in society, law, and politics.
republic: A government in which a country's citizens hold political power.

savanna: Large area of arid grassland with sparse trees and bushes.
settler: White, non-Kenyan people encouraged to emigrate to Kenya in the first decades of the 20th century.
socialism: An economic and political system where goods and industry are state owned and where the economy is planned.
Swahili: The culture of the east African coast, a mix of African, Arabian, Indian, and European influences. Also the language which originated from this culture.

temperate: Description of climate that has mild temperatures and moderate, fairly even rainfall.
trade balance: The difference between the sum a country earns from exports and earns from imports.
trading winds: Seasonal winds, especially those in the Indian Ocean which were used by traders to carry them between Africa, Arabia, and India.

Uhuru: Freedom or independence, particularly that of Kenya in 1963.

Bibliography

Major Sources Used for This Book

Knappert, Jan. *East Africa: Kenya, Tanzania, and Uganda.* London: Vikas Pub., 1987.

Odhiambo, E. S. Atieno. *History of East Africa.* New York: Longman, 1978.

Were, Gideon S, Wilson, Derek, A. *East Africa Through a Thousand Years.* New York: Africana Pub., 1987.

CIA World Factbook 1998 (www.odci.gov/cia/publications/factbook)

General Further Reading

Encyclopedia of World Cultures ed. Lynda A. Bennett. Boston: G.K. Hall, 1992.

The Kingfisher History Encyclopedia. New York: Kingfisher, 1999.

Student Atlas. New York: Dorling Kindersley, 1998.

The World Book Encyclopedia. Chicago: Scott Fetzer Company, 1999.

World Reference Atlas Dorling Kindersley, London, 2000.

Further Reading About Kenya

Kenya, Joel. *Kenya in Pictures (Visual Geography Series).* Minneapolis: Lerner Publications Company, 1997.

King, David C. *Kenya: Let's All Pull Together.* Estes Park, CO: Benchmark Books, 1997.

Maxon, Robert M. *East Africa: An Introductory History.* West Virginia University Press, 1994.

Heritage Library of African Peoples, East Africa (Series). New York: Rosen Publishing Group, 1994–1996

Some Websites About Kenya

www.kenyaembassy.com (Kenyan Embassy in Washington, D.C.)

www.kenyaweb.com

www.museums.or.ke (National Museums of Kenya)

www.naturekenya.org

Index

Page numbers in *italics* refer to pictures or their captions.

Acknowledgments

Cover Photo Credits
Kenyan Tourist Board: Samburu woman, Rift Valley;
Werner Forman Archive: Rhino carving

Photo Credits
Corbis: 25, Chinch Gryniewicz 37, David G. Houser
39, Carl Purcell 38, Jeffery L. Rotman 114, Liba
Taylor 111, David Turnley 79, Werner Forman 95;
Empics: Neal Simpson 104;
Hulton Getty: 66, 69; **Hutchison Library:** Crispin
Hughs 87; **Images of Africa Photobank:** Carla
Signorini Jones 27, David Keith Jones 1, 18, 19, 21,
23, 28, 31, 32, 35, 36, 40, 42, 43, 44, 46, 53, 55, 72,
73, 83, 90, 94, 96, 98, 103, 107, 110; **Kenyan
Tourist Board:** 6, 12, 16, 17, 22, 29, 88, 92, 99, 101,
102, 108, 113, 116; **Mary Evans Picture Library:** 61,
63; **Robert Hunt Library:** 64, 68, 70, 71; **Still
Pictures:** 97, Ron Giling 76, 80, Jorgan Schytte 105;
Werner Forman Archive: 57, 59